SAY IT LOUD

SAY IT

LOUD

An Illustrated History of the Black Athlete

Roxanne Jones and Jessie Paolucci

Foreword by Tony Dungy

ESPN
BOOKS

BALLANTINE BOOKS
NEW YORK

For Malcolm, my sunshine.
—R.J.

For Gary, who taught me to read, write, and
snoop for the surprising in every story.
—J.P.

Published in the United States by ESPN Books, an imprint of ESPN, Inc., New York, and Ballantine Books, an imprint of The Random House Publishing Group, a division of Random House, Inc., New York.

BALLANTINE and colophon are registered trademarks of Random House, Inc. The ESPN Books name and logo are registered trademarks of ESPN, Inc.

Photography and illustration credits can be found on page 245.

Library of Congress Cataloging-in-Publication Data:

Jones, Roxanne.
   Say it loud : an illustrated history of the Black athlete / Roxanne Jones and Jessie Paolucci ; foreword by Tony Dungy.
       p. cm.
   Includes bibliographical references.
   ISBN 978-0-345-51589-6 (hardcover)
  1. African American athletes--History. 2. African American athletes--History--Pictorial works. 3. African American athletes--Biography. 4. African American athletes--Biography--Pictorial works. I. Paolucci, Jessie. II. Title.
   GV706.32.J66 2010
   796.08996073--dc22
                            2010015014

Printed in China

www.ballantinebooks.com
www.espnbooks.com

9 8 7 6 5 4 3 2 1

First Edition

Book design by Henry Lee Studio

I did not take up this work for my own benefit but for those of my race who need help. The work is now well started and I know God will raise up others to take care of the future.

—Harriet Tubman

Say it loud—I'm black and I'm proud!

—James Brown

FOREWORD BY TONY DUNGY

I was honored when asked to write an introduction to *Say It Loud* because this book covers two topics I am very passionate about—sports and African-American history. It chronicles the achievements of men and women who were not only sports icons, but who also sought to do more than just win on the field. These heroes were committed to using their abilities to not only make their sport better, but to make America better as well.

Today we see so many African-Americans enjoying success in so many sports, we sometimes take for granted the tough path some of our pioneers had to travel to make it all possible. For every Venus or Serena Williams, there is an Althea Gibson, who won in the 1950s when no African-Americans were playing in major tennis tournaments. Tiger Woods may be the most recognized athlete in the world today, but he may not have taken up golf had it not been for the efforts of Charlie Sifford and Lee Elder, men who broke down the color barrier on the PGA Tour.

I have a son who will be playing college football in 2010 at Oregon, but he could do it at any school in the country.

I sometimes remind him that I played with the first black scholarship players at Florida State and Alabama, and there was a time when he would not have been allowed to play at those schools. In those days, it was the Historically Black Colleges and Universities that nurtured many of our African-American athletes. They were guided by legendary coaches, such as Grambling's Eddie Robinson in football, Winston-Salem's Clarence "Big House" Gaines in basketball, and Ed Temple, who led the Tennessee State Tigerbelles track and field team. These were brilliant coaches who never got the national recognition they deserved but left an unforgettable mark on their sport.

Like those HBCU coaches, there is another group of men who should be household names in sports history but are not because of the politics of their era—the Negro Leagues baseball players. Some of the greatest athletes to ever play the game will never be in the major league record books, but that doesn't diminish their abilities or contributions. Would men like Satchel Paige, Josh Gibson, and "Cool Papa" Bell have put up the same kinds of numbers

Before coaching the Indianapolis Colts to victory in Super Bowl XLI, and becoming the first African-American to do so, Dungy was a safety for the Super Bowl XIII-winning Pittsburgh Steelers.

that Walter Johnson, Babe Ruth, and Ty Cobb did in the majors? Many historians think they would have. But in spite of not getting the chance they deserved, they opened the door for such players as Willie Mays and Hank Aaron, who in turn inspired many of the stars of my generation.

Black athletes were pioneers in many sports, in ways we can't even relate to today. We wouldn't think of a player-coach now, but Bill Russell and Lenny Wilkens did it in the NBA, and Fritz Pollard did it in professional football. And they did it at a championship level. It's hard to imagine, but there was a time when many of the great jockeys were African-American, and it wasn't unusual to see men like Isaac Murphy and Jimmy Winkfield in the winner's circle at the Kentucky Derby.

This book not only looks at the pioneers but also remembers those athletes who used their platforms to make social and legal changes, even if it meant putting their careers in jeopardy. I think of Muhammed Ali being stripped of his heavyweight championship because he stood up for his religious beliefs. Men like Curt Flood in baseball and John

Mackey in football, who risked being blackballed because they wouldn't stand for systems that prevented athletes from selling their services on an open market, thus opening the door for the free agency and salaries that today's athletes enjoy. I believe that's the true measure of greatness in sports—when the actions of athletes transcend the playing field and affect the way we live.

Say It Loud is a wonderful look at our history in athletics, covering well over a century of African-American achievement in a variety of sports. It's important to remember these great men and women and their achievements because, as we reflect on what they have done, it gives us the ability to dream about the future and to dream about the impact the next generation of African-American athletes can have, on and off the field.

CONTENTS

Jackie Robinson: The First at second.

SAY IT LOUD

FOOTBALL

➡ **SHOOTING THE GAP** ⬅

African-American ballers, from Fritz Pollard to Walter Payton

to Jerry Rice, have been tackling discrimination on the field

with nothing less than a full-on blitz.

Walter Payton
Toward the end of his
sweet career with the
Chicago Bears, Payton
had plenty to smile about.

FIRST AND FOREMOST

Fritz Pollard (1894–1986)

Fritz Pollard, one of the gridiron's earliest and speediest backs, was so fast, and so far ahead of his time, that it took the NFL some 70 years to catch up to him. His litany of historical firsts starts in 1916: As a Brown University freshman, he became the first African-American to play in the Rose Bowl, and as a sophomore, he led the Bears to their first football win over Harvard.

After graduation in 1919 and a stint in the Army, Pollard joined the Akron Pros, leading them to the first championship of the American Pro Football Association (the forerunner to the NFL) in his rookie season. In 1921, he was named Akron's player-coach, making him the first and the last African-American to helm an NFL team until Art Shell was named the Raiders head coach 67 years later. When Pollard signed with the Hammond Pros in 1923, he shifted to what would later be defined as the quarterback spot—the first and only black quarterback in pro football until Willie Thrower took a snap for the Bears in 1953.

In later life, Pollard founded the *New York Independent News*, served as president of Harlem's Suntan Movie Studio, and became an agent for such stars as Paul Robeson. In 1954 he did finally come in second, joining previous inductee Duke Slater as the only African-Americans in the College Football Hall of Fame.

In 1916, the Brown University freshman became the first black player in the Rose Bowl. And he was just getting started.

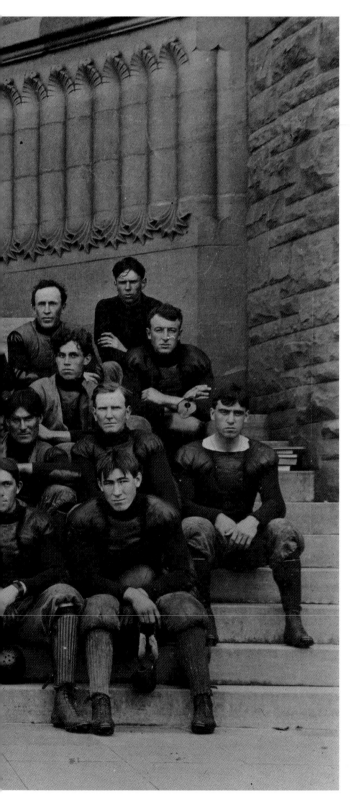

THE STANDOUT

Bobby Marshall (1880–1958)

Bobby Marshall (second row from bottom, second from the left) was more than a black face in the white crowd at the University of Minnesota. From 1904 to 1906, the future College Football Hall of Fame end helped lead the Gophers to a 27-2 record while they outscored foes 1,238-63. If highlight reels existed in his era, his game-winning 60-yard field goal against Chicago in 1906 would be at the top of the list. The first black football player in the Big Nine (later the Big Ten), Marshall also competed in baseball, track, hockey, and boxing at Minnesota. He graduated with a law degree, but chose to play pro football in Minnesota. From 1920 to 1924, he was one of just a handful of black players in the NFL. Marshall ended his football career with the Rock Island Independents at the age of 44, though he did appear in an exhibition game six years later.

In 1921, Slater and his Hawkeyes laid down some law: They denied Knox College even one first down, slapped Notre Dame with its first loss in two years, and defeated Illinois in front of 15,000 on their way to the Western Conference title.

FIELD JUDGE

Fred "Duke" Slater (1898–1966)

Twenty-five years before Jackie Robinson integrated baseball, Duke Slater tackled the color line in pro football. The first black All-American at the University of Iowa dominated the tackle position in the pros from 1922 to 1931, playing for the Rock Island Independents, Milwaukee Badgers, and Chicago Cardinals. The 6'1", 215-pound intimidator was feared on the field and revered for his quick mind off it. Slater returned to Iowa's law school during his off-seasons, earning his degree in 1928. When he retired from the Cardinals in 1931, he was appointed assistant district attorney in Chicago, and in 1948 he won a Chicago municipal court judgeship by an overwhelming majority. In 1951 he became the first African-American elected to the College Football Hall of Fame, but the Pro Football Hall of Fame has yet to recognize his place in the game.

RUNNING START

Jerome "Brud" Holland (1916–1985)

Jerome "Brud" Holland got things done. In 1935, Brud was Cornell University's first African-American to play football and one of its greatest players. The 6-foot, 215-pound offensive end was a legend on campus. Alumni born far too late to have seen Holland play still crow about his three touchdowns in the fourth quarter of a 40–7 drubbing over Colgate in 1937.

But football wasn't Holland's only claim to greatness. After earning his PhD in sociology at the University of Pennsylvania, the two-time All-America was eventually named president of Delaware State University and later Hampton Institute. In 1970, President Richard Nixon appointed Holland ambassador to Sweden, and in 1972 Holland became the first African-American to serve on the board of the New York Stock Exchange.

In 1985, Ronald Reagan posthumously awarded Holland the Presidential Medal of Freedom for his contributions to education and public service.

LOADED FOR BEAR

George Taliaferro (b.1927)

As a kid growing up in the 1930s in Gary, Indiana, George Taliaferro told everyone he knew that nothing would ever stop him from playing football for the Chicago Bears. In his wildest dreams he never imagined he'd actually turn down the chance. Twice.

Taliaferro started his football career as a fierce two-way back for Indiana University, leading the Hoosiers to an undefeated season and their first Big Ten conference championship in 1945 while earning a first team All-America spot as a halfback. Four years later, legendary Bears owner George Halas ignored the NFL's color barrier to make him the league's first African-American draft pick, but Taliaferro declined; he'd already signed a contract to play for the Los Angeles Dons in the All-America Football Conference. His word was more important than the opportunity to fulfill his childhood dream. After the AAFC folded in 1950, the NFL came calling again, but it was the New York Yankees who snapped him up. Over the next six seasons Taliaferro gained 1,794 rushing yards with the Yanks, Texans, Colts, and Eagles, and was chosen for the 1951, 1952, and 1953 Pro Bowls before retiring from football in 1955.

Halas, however, had other plans for the back who got away. Still impressed by Taliaferro's integrity back in 1949, Halas offered him a spot on the 1955 Bears team. Although only in his late 20s, Taliaferro knew he was past his prime and felt it wouldn't be fair to take Papa Bear's money.

Taliaferro never did play for his beloved Bears, but he always led the league in integrity.

TOUGH LOVE

Eddie Robinson (1919–2007)

Eddie Robinson, head coach of Grambling State University from 1941 until 1997, retired as the winningest coach in college football history. Over 55 seasons, Robinson led Grambling to 408 victories and captured 17 Southwestern Athletic Conference championships. More than 200 of his players matriculated to the NFL, including Hall of Famers Willie Brown and Buck Buchanan. But for Coach Rob, education was far more important than Xs and Os. "If a boy can't tackle, we show him how," Robinson once wrote. "But I sometimes wondered if anybody cared enough to teach them to read."

To ensure his charges kept their noses in their textbooks as often as their playbooks, Robinson demanded report cards from his players. And God help the baller who missed so much as one class. Endless bleacher sprints and missed meals tended to keep class-cutting to a minimum. Doug Williams, who would become the first black quarterback to win a Super Bowl, credits one late-night recruiting call for his future success. "In the wee hours the phone rings," recalled Williams, who would replace Robinson as Grambling's coach in 1998. "[My mother] told me I was going to Grambling. 'Coach Robinson said you were going to go to church, you were to go to class, and you were going to graduate,' and the case was closed."

Robinson didn't just make football players. Before walking away after 57 years at Grambling, he made them all men.

GAME-CHANGER

Jim Brown (**b.1936**)

Arguably the greatest athlete of his day, Jim Brown was certainly the finest running back the NFL had ever seen. A four-sport star at Syracuse University (football, lacrosse, basketball, track), he was selected sixth overall by the Cleveland Browns in the 1957 draft and made an immediate impact with his brute force, speed, and agility. In seven of his nine seasons, he rushed for over 1,000 yards, and his 1,863 yards (in 14 games) in 1963 is still the franchise record. Brown quit the game at the age of 29 to pursue a movie career (that's him above left with Raquel Welch in *100 Rifles*), but multiple domestic violence incidents tarnished his image. To his credit, Brown has devoted much of his third act to community work, helping to rehabilitate gang members and prisoners and mentoring athletes.

Even as a rookie in 1957, Brown was a handful for opponents like the New York Giants.

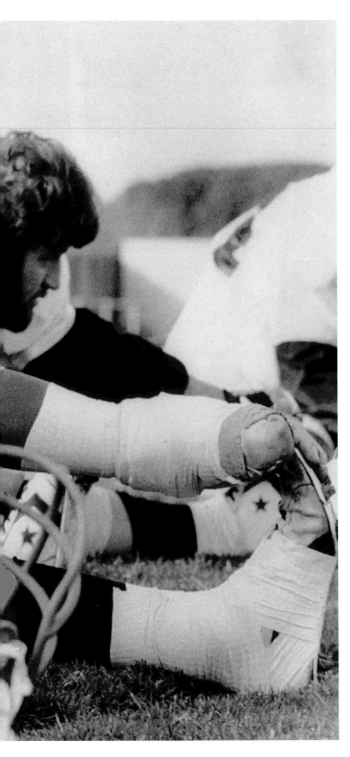

CIVIL GUARD

Gene Upshaw (1945–2008)

If it's lonely at the top, former NFL Players Association head Gene Upshaw never showed it. Maybe it was because he still had a long career's worth of applause ringing in his ears. The 6'5", 255-pound left guard from Texas A&I University was the Raiders' first-round draft pick in 1967, the first year of the combined AFL-NFL draft. He earned his Hall of Fame spot with 10 AFL and AFC title games, two Super Bowl rings, and seven Pro Bowls. Upshaw was ferocious and fiercely smart on the field. An exceptional leader, he served as team captain and union representative for 13 years. After retiring in 1983, he was elected executive director of the NFL Players Association.

Often maligned for being too cozy with the NFL management, Upshaw nonetheless turned the once anemic union into a stronghold. He guided the players through contentious players strikes in 1982 and 1987. And in 2006 he negotiated a lucrative six-year extension of the collective bargaining agreement that netted players a 59.5% share of the league's total revenue. With it, he brokered a salary cap increase that, by 2007, allotted $109 million per team. At his funeral service in 2008, former NFL commissioner Paul Tagliabue said, "I've never had a better rival, teammate, or friend."

He protected quarterbacks and running backs as a player, and players as executive director of the NFL Players Association.

COMEBACK ROUTE

Marlin Briscoe (b.1945)

Nicknamed The Magician, Marlin Briscoe's toughest trick was actually breaking his addiction to cocaine. His career, however, was no sleight of hand—his accomplishments were hard-won and well-earned. A standout QB at Omaha University, Briscoe graduated with 5,114 passing yards and 22 school records. Yet when the Denver Broncos drafted him in 1968, he was placed in the defensive backfield. Only after QB Steve Tensi broke his collarbone and backup Jim LeClair failed did Briscoe become the first black starting QB in the AFL—and pro football history.

It didn't last. Though he did pass for 1,589 yards and 14 TDs in 11 games, Briscoe's completion percentage (41.5%) was too low, and he was told the following season that he was too small for the spot. He'd never quarterback again. Instead, he jumped to the Buffalo Bills, where he enjoyed three stellar seasons as a wide receiver, once leading the AFC in receptions. Three years later, he earned his first of two Super Bowl rings with Miami, before retiring in 1976.

But his biggest battle was ahead of him: ending a 10-year crack addiction. Today, Briscoe is back in charge, working at the Watts/Willowbrook Boys and Girls Club, a safe haven for kids in one of Los Angeles' roughest neighborhoods.

The Magician was the first black quarterback in the pre-merger NFL, but the real trick was the way he made his addiction to drugs vanish.

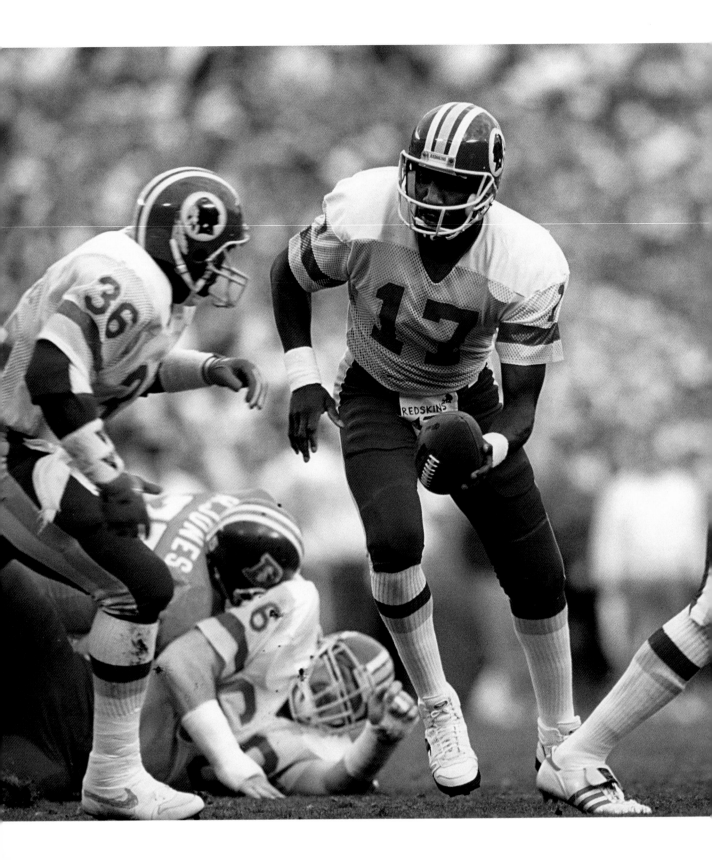

Alan Page (b.1945)

One of the greatest defensive tackles in NFL history, Page was named the league MVP for 1971—the first defensive player to win the honor. In 15 seasons in the NFL, he made nine Pro Bowls, recovered 23 fumbles, blocked 28 kicks, and had 173 sacks. His ability to analyze every side of the game served him very well: Page was elected to both the Pro Football Hall of Fame and a seat on the Minnesota Supreme Court.

Doug Williams (b.1955)

Thanks to Williams (No. 17), the Redskins clobbered John Elway's Broncos 42-10 in Super Bowl XXII. He completed 18 of 29 passes for 340 yards (including an 80-yarder to Ricky Sanders) and four TDs. Williams topped off the day with a Super Bowl XXII MVP award. He is still the only black QB to win a Super Bowl.

←

PREVIOUS PAGE

Walter Payton
(1954–1999)

The Bears' great running back was equally impressive on his feet and in the air (soaring here against Tampa Bay in 1981). Payton defied gravity and defined grace, on and off the field. When he retired after the 1987 season, he had 125 career touchdowns and 16,726 rushing yards—the all-time record until Emmitt Smith surpassed it in 2002.

Franco Harris
(b.1950)

Harris immediately became Pittsburgh's favorite son after he was drafted in 1972. In his rookie season, he was on the receiving end of the most divine play in the history of football: the Immaculate Reception pass from Terry Bradshaw that gave the Steelers' their first-ever playoff win, a 13-7 victory against the Raiders. For his winged feet and magic touch, as well as his 24 points and 354 rushing yards in four Super Bowls, Harris was enshrined in the Hall of Fame in 1990. After he retired, he took over the historic Parks Sausage Company—the first black-owned public company in the U.S. when it offered stock in 1969.

Jerry Rice (b.1962)
November 14, 1993, was a
better-than-average day
at the office for Rice. Here,
the eventual all-time leader
in nearly every category for
wide receivers scores his
fourth touchdown of the day
against Tampa Bay.

**Reggie White
(1961–2004)**
The Minister of Defense
squashes Shannon Sharpe as
the two scramble for a Broncos
fumble during the Packers
41-6 win in December 1996.
When White retired, or rather
re-retired, in 2000, he was
the NFL's all-time leader in
sacks with 198. As an ordained
evangelical minister, White
was also an inspirational voice
throughout the league.

BLACKBALLED

Paul Robeson (1898–1976)

"An artist must elect to fight for freedom or slavery. I have made my choice. I had no alternative." Paul Robeson was the most rarefied kind of genius: jack-of-all-trades and master of all. He was a multilingual scholar and a world-class baritone, a civil rights activist and a Shakespearean actor—and, incidentally, an All-America athlete. He achieved greatness in every classical sense. Yet the fight he chose, because it labeled him red as well as black, rendered this Renaissance man a figure of tragedy, alienated from his public if not his art.

Robeson's virtuosity was first spotlighted on the football field at Rutgers University, where he earned a four-year academic scholarship in 1915. As the first African-American football player in the school's history, he was subjected to racist assaults from his own teammates, and he tenaciously fought back. In one scrimmage, the 6'3", 191-pound lineman was attacked so viciously that he was removed from the field with two broken ribs, a dislocated shoulder, and a broken nose. Undaunted, Robeson returned to play several days later. "I made a tackle and was on the ground, my right palm down on the ground," Robeson told *The New York Times* in 1944. "A boy came over and stepped hard on my hand. His cleats took every single one of my fingernails off my right hand. That's when I knew rage! The next play the whole first-string backfield came at me. I swept out my arms, and the three men running interference went down. I got Kelly [the ballcarrier] in my two hands and I got him over my head ... I was going to smash him so hard to the ground that I'd break him in two, and I could

"Do you mean a party of people who have sacrificed for my people, and for all Americans and workers, that they can live in dignity?"

—Paul Robeson

have done it. But just then the coach yelled, 'Robey, you're on the varsity!'"

It was a decision coach George Foster Sanford and his squad did not regret. In the 31 games Rutgers played while Robeson was on the team, the Scarlet Knights outscored opponents 944 to 191. Playing both offense and defense, Robeson was indomitable . In 1917 Rutgers beat the undefeated Newport Naval team 14–0, thanks in large part to Robeson's defense and his touchdown pass reception. When Walter Camp, "The Father of American Football," selected Robeson as an All-America in 1918 for a second time, he called him "a veritable superman."

Sports greatness hardly exempted Robeson from racism. His locker was segregated from his teammates', and during away games, he was forced to stay in black-only hotel rooms. After his freshman year, he was banned from the school's annual football banquet. In his sophomore year, Washington and Lee University threatened to cancel its game at Rutgers if Robeson wasn't benched. Coach Sanford relented that time, but wouldn't make the mistake again. When West Virginia made the same demand, Sanford refused.

After graduating as valedictorian in 1919, Robeson was signed by the Akron Pros of the American Professional Football Association. But his three APFA years (he also played for Hammond, Indiana, and Milwaukee) were only a means to an end: He was using his $500 per game salary to pay his way through Columbia Law School. Robeson wouldn't practice law for long either—he quit the New York City law firm Stotesbury and Miner after a secretary refused to take dictation from him. For a black man in New York in the 1920s—the era of the Harlem Renaissance—the arts held out the best opportunity for self- expression and Robeson soon found himself on the stage. He commuted between drama (Eugene O'Neill's *Emperor Jones* in 1924) and Broadway musicals like *Showboat*. (He would have to go to London, in 1930, to play Othello.)

The son of a former slave, Robeson had always been outspoken about racial injustice. But after he performed in Russia in late 1934, Robeson's activism became defined by the ideological compass of the period. In the 1930s Robeson aligned himself with the Communist Party, and in 1950 his passport was revoked. Brought before the House Un-American Activities Committee in 1956, he refused to acknowledge the legitimacy of the committee invoking the Fifth Amendment on questions regarding his Communist affiliation. ("Do you mean a party of people who have sacrificed for my people, and for all Americans and workers, that they can live in dignity?") Robeson's passport was restored in 1958, though he was always under surveillance. He performed abroad, only to return reportedly broken and depressed. He was not forgotten though. A 75th birthday celebration for Robeson was held at Carnegie Hall, and while illness kept him from attending, he did send this message: "Though I have not been able to be active for several years, I want you to know that I am the same Paul, dedicated as ever to the worldwide cause of humanity for freedom, peace, and brotherhood."

TURNING
THE TIDE

Ozzie Newsome (b.1956)

Ozzie Newsome is a veteran at being first. He was the first freshman receiver to start under famed coach Bear Bryant at Alabama. And he was the first African-American general manager of an NFL team. But for this Hall of Famer from Muscle Shoals, Alabama, nothing was as difficult as being one of the first black kids to integrate his small-town grade school. "One thing I learned about going to that predominantly white school was to bite my tongue and be patient," Newsome told *The Baltimore Sun* in 2000. "When you go through something like that at age 12, there are very few things that rattle you."

On the field, nothing much ever fazed him. The star wide receiver at Colbert County High was so heavily recruited that Coach Bryant gave his recruiter, John Mitchell, strict orders not to return without Newsome's commitment letter. Mitchell, now the defensive line coach for the Steelers, recalled to *The Sun*, "I ate breakfast with his family. I went to class with him all day ... and around midnight, his mom said it was about time for me to go home. I said, 'Ma'am, no disrespect to you, but Coach Bryant told me not to let him out of my sight, so if you don't mind, I'd like to sleep on your sofa.'" The young gun turned out to be well worth the effort. An All-America, Newsome made 102 career receptions for 2,070 yards for Bama. Bryant quickly dubbed him the Wizard of Oz. The respect was mutual. "[Coach Bryant] was one of the first in the South to recruit black players," Newsome said. "He taught me the importance of team. He believed that you had to improve 10% every day."

> ## "His passion for the game, that's his legacy."
>
> *—Herm Edwards*

When he was drafted in the first round by the Browns in 1978, the 6'2", 232-pounder switched to tight end and redefined the position. In 13 NFL seasons, Newsome caught more passes than any tight end ever had before, with 662 for 7,980 yards and 47 TDs. On the last 557 touches or possessions of his career, Newsome didn't fumble once.

Impressed by his work ethic and nimble leadership, Browns owner Art Modell hired Newsome as a scout in 1991. Five years later, Modell asked him to take the reins as vice president of player personnel. It was a difficult career choice for Newsome; Modell had just moved the beloved Browns to Baltimore in the middle of the night, leaving behind legions of angry fans. Although heartbroken by the move, Newsome nonetheless felt that Modell was a decent man. By accepting the job, Newsome became the highest-ranked African-American in the NFL at the time. As VP, and six years later as the league's first black GM, Newsome built the fledgling Baltimore Ravens into a powerhouse. In 2001, just five years after the Wizard of Oz began working his magic behind the scenes, the Ravens crushed the Giants 34-7 in the Ravens' first Super Bowl appearance.

Herm Edwards, then the Chiefs head coach, said Newsome's long list of firsts pales in comparison to his less tangible accomplishments. "More than catching passes and going into the Hall of Fame," Edwards said, "he's trying to always make his players, his coaches, the game better. His passion for the game, that's his legacy."

Newsome redefined the tight end position, snatching 662 career passes for 47 TDs.

BASKETBALL

➡ LEAPS AND BOUNDS ⬅

Thanks to teachers like Dr. Edwin Henderson, titans like Bill

Russell, and talents like Magic Johnson, African-Americans

have dominated the hardwood—and made a lasting impact on

the culture at large.

Earvin "Magic" Johnson
Magic arrived in the NBA in 1979 with
an infectious personality and the gifts,
at 6'9", to magically revolutionize the
point guard position.

ROVING MAESTROS

New York Renaissance (1922–1949)

Before million-dollar contracts and players' unions; before the ABA, the NBA, or the NCAA; before a black man could drink from a white water fountain, the New York Renaissance was one of the most indomitable forces in professional sports. For 27 years after its founding in 1922, the Rens faced off against any club willing to play them, and in the process amassed a staggering 2,588–529 record. Winning, however, was the easy part. With up to 90 road games in often 120–game seasons, the league-less Rens blitzed America, sometimes attracting more than 15,000 fans to a game. And along the way they were treated to every conceivable kind of racism: fleabag hotels, back-alley slop shops, slurs, riots, and death threats.

From the team's inception, owner Bob Douglas envisioned a revolution in team play and sniffed out the nation's best ball-handlers: should-be legends like forward Eyre Saitch from DeWitt Clinton High in the Bronx; Charles "Tarzan" Cooper out of Philadelphia, one of the first true big men of the game; lightning-footed floor general Clarence "Fats" Jenkins from Commerce High in New York City; John "Boy Wonder" Issacs from New York City; Bill Yancey, who doubled as a shortstop in the Negro Leagues; and James "Pappy" Ricks, a deadly forward from the Loendi Big Five.

Red Holzman, the renowned Knicks coach who grew up going to Rens games, told Harvey Frommer in his book *Holzman on Hoops* that the Rens enlightened his

Charles "Tarzan" Cooper (1907–1980)
From 1929 to 1941, Cooper's uncanny rebounding and tidy ignition of the
fast break were the linchpins in the Rens' unstoppable game.

The 1939 Rens were more than snappy dressers. They also won the inaugural pro basketball world championship in a drubbing of the Oshkosh All-Stars of the all-white National Basketball League.

view of the game. "On courts they were unfamiliar with, in all kinds of strange places, the Rens played great team basketball. They specialized in a switching, man-to-man defense. It held the opposition's scoring down and it also saved them steps and energy."

Holzman was not the only fan. The Original Celtics, considered the premier team of the era, had enormous respect for the Rens. And for good reason: They won 88 consecutive games in an 86-day stretch in the 1932-33 season. In 1939 they won the *Chicago Herald-American*'s inaugural World Professional Basketball Tournament, the first all-black team to win a world title.

But the perpetual harassment took a toll. In *Elevating the Game* by Nelson George, owner Douglas recounted a particularly ugly incident when the Original Celtics came out to watch a Rens game in Louisville. "Joe Lapchick [the Celts' center] ran out on the court and embraced Tarzan Cooper because he was so glad to see him," said Douglas. "There was silence on the court. This was Jim Crow country, and the races were strictly separated. The Celtics were put out of their hotel and a riot was narrowly averted."

Even after 20 years of crushing nearly every team they encountered, the Rens still couldn't break through the racial barrier. When the owners from the newly formed Basketball Association of America met in 1946 to discuss admitting the Rens to the league, the answer was no. Lapchick, then with the Knicks, reportedly said before the vote, "I may lose my job saying this, but I'd play against the Rens any goddamn day. To me, they're the best." The Rens were denied entry, but Lapchick kept his job and went one step further. In 1950, as coach of the Knicks, he signed the NBA's first black player: Nat "Sweetwater" Clifton.

In their last season in 1948-49, having relocated to Ohio, the Rens were admitted into the National Basketball League as the Dayton Rens, the first all-black team to play in a pro sports league. While history has largely forgotten them, the Rens did get some measure of recognition: They were inducted into the Basketball Hall of Fame in 1963.

TRICKY BUSINESS

Harlem Globetrotters (b.1926)

Their kooky passes and trampoline tricks, not to mention their .985 won-lost percentage against mainly cooperative opponents in more than 25,000 games, always masked major basketball talent. Founded in 1926, and bought by Abe Saperstein in 1928, the Globetrotters were not always court jesters. In fact, they were nearly as feared as the New York Renaissance—at least in the early barnstorming days. Playing close to 100 games a year, the Globetrotters developed a winning strategy for every kind of competitor, though not a way to beat discrimination. In Robert W. Peterson's *Cages to Jump Shots: Pro Basketball's Early Years*, Bernie Price, who played center for the Trotters in the '30s and '40s recalled, "In some small towns the kids had never seen blacks before, and they would rub our skins to see if the black would rub off. We were treated badly everywhere."

The Globetrotters ran up such humiliating scores that teams eventually began to balk at playing them. The remedy? Design ball gymnastics, now their trademark, to slow down scoring and keep crowds happy. After playing in front of 130 million fans in 120 countries, it's hard to knock them for still making people smile.

As Louis Pressley illustrates here in 1951, the balance between entertainment and ability was at the heart of the Harlem Globetrotters' mission.

FORWARD MARCH

Earl Lloyd (b.1928)

Chuck Cooper may have been the first African-American drafted by an NBA team (Celtics, second round, 1950), and Nat "Sweetwater" Clifton may have been the first to sign an NBA contract (Knicks, May 24, 1950), but it was Earl "The Big Cat" Lloyd who made history by being the first to actually step onto the NBA hardwood during a game. After being picked up in the ninth round by the Washington Capitols, Lloyd made his debut on October 31, 1950, in the season opener against the Rochester Royals. The event involved a poignant personal first for Lloyd as well. "To that point," he told *The Washington Times* in 1999, "I had never sat next to or even talked to a white person before." The 6'8" power forward developed his strong D and sharp picks at West Virginia State College, shutting down opponents as the Yellow Jackets won consecutive Central Intercollegiate Athletic Association titles in 1948 and 1949. Though Lloyd says his NBA peers were never anything but welcoming, some fans were not so receptive. During the Capitols' third game of the 1950 season, at home against Minneapolis, his parents endured scathing racial taunts by white spectators, and after a game against Fort Wayne, Indiana, Lloyd and a white teammate were spit on as they walked off the court arm in arm. For black athletes in pre-Civil Rights Era America, it was all, unfortunately, in a day's work.

Three years after he became the first black player in the NBA, Lloyd was still on the defensive. With the Syracuse Nationals, Lloyd blocks Nelson Bobb's layup.

John McLendon
(1915–1999)

In 1934, the 19-year-old McLendon, a physical education major at the University of Kansas, was walking through the gym with his advisor, basketball inventor and Kansas basketball program founder Dr. James Naismith. Naismith told McLendon, "Wherever the ball is, is where the offense begins." McLendon, whose race prevented him from playing for the university, had a eureka moment and envisioned the fast break, which he developed, along with the four-corner offense, in the 1940s. After arranging, at great personal risk, for secret games between his North Carolina College for Negroes teams and white schools, he was instrumental in integrating both the NAIA and NCAA tournaments. In 1960, he became the first black coach in any integrated professional league when George Steinbrenner hired him to coach the short-lived Cleveland Pipers of the American Basketball League.

Cheesing for the camera in December 1950, Kellogg did not know that six weeks later he would blow the whistle on perhaps the biggest scandal in college basketball history.

THE INSIDER

Junius Kellogg (1927–1998)

With all the controversies swirling around today's sports, it's easy to forget the traumatic lessons of 1951, when a kid from Manhattan College risked his career to blow the whistle on the biggest betting scandal in NCAA history.

A World War II veteran, Junius Kellogg made an immediate impact at Manhattan College, where he enrolled under the G.I. Bill in 1950. Not only was the 6'8" big man the school's first African-American basketball player, he was also the Jaspers' first scholarship athlete. As the biggest inside threat on the team, Kellogg was a game-changer. To skew the odds for racketeer Cornelius Kelleher, former teammate Henry Poppe tried to convince Kellogg to take a dive in their January 17, 1951, game against DePaul. Kellogg told *Newsday* in 1998, "He offered me $1,000. I told him to get the hell out of my room." Afraid of losing his college eligibility, Kellogg reported the bribe to Jaspers coach Ken Norton, who called the police. Kellogg agreed to wear a wire in a meeting with gamblers, where he pretended to have reconsidered. After Manhattan College squelched the bookies in a sweet three-point defeat of DePaul, the police swooped in and arrested Poppe and former Manhattan co-captain John Byrnes, among others.

Over the next year, 30 more college players from CCNY, LIU, Bradley, NYU, Kentucky, and Toledo were implicated in the point-shaving scandals.

Kellogg graduated in 1953 and joined the Harlem Globetrotters. While on tour in 1954, Kellogg was paralyzed in a car accident, though he eventually regained the use of his hands and arms. Later, he coached the Pan Am Jets to four International Wheelchair Basketball championships and was named a deputy commissioner for community development for New York City.

PREVIOUS PAGE
The Big O grabs a rebound in high style against Kansas State during the 1959 NCAA tourney, while Bob Boozer (right) watches.

SUPERNATURAL

Oscar Robertson (b.1938)

Oscar Robertson, the man who racked up the NBA's only triple-double season and the player Red Auerbach said "is so great, he scares me," was unstoppable from the start. Instead of playing baseball, the more popular game in the Indianapolis housing project where he grew up, 6-year-old Oscar tossed rubber band-bound rags into a peach basket. At the University of Cincinnati, where he endured racism as the college's first black player, Robertson revolutionized the one-handed shot, scoring 33.8 points per game and leading the Bearcats to a 79–9 record in his three years on the team. In the NBA, the first true big guard revolutionized the fadeaway jumper and driving layup. After 10 years on the Cincinnati Royals, the Big O was traded in 1970 to Milwaukee, which immediately won the NBA championship.

Robertson wasn't done rewriting the books. In 1970, as the head of the players union, he filed a landmark antitrust suit against the NBA that challenged the league's free agency rules and stalled the merger of the ABA and the NBA. Six years later, the league settled after agreeing to forego compensation for teams who lost free agents, effectively freeing up more money for player salaries.

After 14 years, 26,710 points, 9,887 assists, and 7,804 rebounds, Robertson retired from basketball in 1974 to open a business in Indianapolis—building quality housing for low-income families.

CLASH OF THE TITANS

Wilt Chamberlain (1936–1999) and Kareem Abdul-Jabbar (b.1947)

It was January 9, 1972, and the torch was soon to be passed. The Lakers had just won their 33rd straight game behind the aging Chamberlain. On this night, the Milwaukee Bucks, led by his heir apparent, Kareem Abdul-Jabbar, snapped the Lakers' streak and set up a prolonged clash of these two titans in the Western Conference Finals that spring. Chamberlain and the Lakers got their revenge, beating the Bucks in six, but for the next 17 years, Jabbar and his sky hook would wreak their own havoc. Before his career was over, Jabbar collected six championship rings (five with the Lakers) and set nine NBA records, including an all-time total of 38,387 points.

With grace and enormous intelligence, Coach Gaines led the Rams to 18 20-win seasons and eight Central Intercollegiate Athletic Association titles.

MASTER BUILDER

Clarence "Big House" Gaines (1923–2005)

"Records come and go, but if you touch people's lives, they'll remember you," Clarence "Big House" Gaines often said. The Winston-Salem State University basketball coach is best known for his 1967 championship squad that included Earl "The Pearl" Monroe—the first historically black college to win an NCAA Division II title in any sport. But that's only one of the reasons he was inducted into the Hall of Fame 11 years before he retired in 1993. More than the high-energy, flashy game he coached, it was Big House's wisdom and kindness that marked his 47-year career. "This giant of a man was really a big teddy bear," eulogized Monroe. "He is responsible for so many of us, not only during our time in school but our lives afterward." There is one record Big House was especially proud of: Nearly 80 percent of his players graduated college.

Walt "Clyde" Frazier (b.1945)

By 1974, Frazier was king of New York. Nicknamed Clyde after famed bank robber Clyde Barrow, Frazier's cool style, dazzling passes, and split-second steals unhinged opponents and turned the Knicks' aggressive defense into high art.

THE MARVEL

Julius "Dr. J" Erving (b.1950)

The seas seemed to part for the miraculous Dr. J., seen here as a skywalking 25-year-old with the New York Nets. He awed crowds with otherworldly hangtime and power slams of the league's equally colorful red-white-and-blue ball. The following year, in 1976, the NBA supposedly bought out the ABA just to lock down the greatest player who ever hit the court. For the next 11 seasons, the Sixers' small forward transformed the game and transfixed its fans with balletic whirls, gravity-defying layups, and his notorious dunks, some of which appeared to come from the free throw line.

Coach Thompson led legions of Hoyas greats into battle, including rookie Patrick Ewing in 1981.

BLUNT FORCE

John Thompson (b.1941)

John Thompson does not mince words. When a reporter asked Georgetown's legendary head coach in 1982 how he felt about becoming the first black coach to reach the Final Four, he shot back, "Other blacks have been denied the right in this country ... I find the question extremely offensive." Two years later, the Hoyas won their first NCAA championship. This time, everyone knew better than to ask him what it felt like to be the first black man to accomplish the feat. From 1972 to 1999, Thompson led the Hoyas to 20 NCAA tournaments, six Big East championships, and three Final Fours. But for the former Boston Celtic, winning took a backseat to social justice. In 1989, Thompson spoke out strenuously against the NCAA's Proposition 42, which denied athletic scholarships to students who did not receive a minimum of 700 on their SATs. In protest, Thompson walked off the court and didn't return until two games later. "What I hope to do is to bring attention to the fact that [Proposition 42] is discriminatory ... SAT scores have proven to be culturally biased." Days later, the NCAA agreed to postpone its decision for further review. When pundits suggested that only someone with a public profile could be so effective, Thompson replied, "Had that been the case, Rosa Parks would still be standing up on that bus. I don't think people stand up because of their position. They have their position because they stand up."

Earvin "Magic" Johnson (b.1959)
In one of the most highly anticipated matchups in college hoops history, Michigan State's Magic Johnson looks to find his man beyond Indiana State's Larry Bird during the 1979 NCAA Finals. Magic's Spartans would beat Bird's Sycamores, 75-64.

WONDER WOMAN

Lusia Harris-Stewart (b.1955)

With averages of 25.9 points and 14.4 rebounds a game, Lusia Harris-Stewart is considered one of the best female centers ever—and her Delta State Unviersity's three national championships and whopping 109-6 record from 1975 to 1977 makes any argument difficult. It shouldn't be any surprise that the 6'3" paint-pounder scored the first-ever point in an Olympic women's basketball game in '76, where she earned a silver medal. Or that she was inducted into the Mississippi Sports Hall of Fame in 1990 and the Naismith Hall of Fame two years later. Or that the New Orleans Jazz picked her in the seventh round of the 1977 draft. Harris-Stewart declined their contract because she had better things to do. Rather than try out, the monster blocker decided to teach special education and coach girls' hoops in Mississippi. Today, despite being wheelchair-bound due to rheumatoid arthritis, Harris-Stewart is still standing tall. Lebron James considers her an inspiration. That, too, is no surprise.

At 6'3", Harris was a head above the rest at the 1976 Olympics.

AIR QUALITY

Michael Jordan (b.1963)

Opponents and teammates weren't the only ones who looked up to His Airness. Over the course of his 15-year career, he accumulated 10 scoring titles, five MVP Awards, 14 All-Star Game appearances, etc., etc., and—perhaps most memorably, along with those images of his tongue-wagging, belief-defying dunks—six NBA titles with the Chicago Bulls.

But his dominance on Chicago's West Madison Street was matched by his unprecedented success on Madison Avenue; armed with a chocolate-smooth bald head, a gold hoop earring, a killer smile, and an equally lethal instinct to be the best, Jordan transformed the branding business as he had a stagnant league. He was the first black athlete to transcend race in the global marketplace, helping a niche company called Nike step all over the competition, then endowing everything from breakfast cereal to underpants with the values he had brought to the game of basketball: intelligence, excellence, determination, and the sense that we could all be better than we are. His flaws—a penchant for gambling, but never on his own sport, and an occasional lapse of graciousness, as in his trash-talking induction speech at the Hall of Fame in 2009—are hardly noticeable in the broad landscape of his brilliant career. In 2010, he won yet another distinction: The first black athlete to become a majority owner of an NBA team, the Charlotte Bobcats.

Be like Mike? Why not try? But being Mike is something only he can do.

DREAM WEAVER

Hakeem Olajuwon (b.1963)

His entire career was something of a dream. The nimble-footed 7-foot center was famous for his unbeatable bob-and-weave move, which became known as the "Dream Shake." Then there was his fantasy season in 1993-94, when he won NBA Defensive Player of the Year and league and Finals MVP honors, as he took the Rockets to their first championship. In 1996 he was a member of the gold-medal-winning Olympic Dream Team. After 18 seasons in the league, The Dream retired with an NBA all-time high of 3,830 blocked shots. On hearing of his likely nomination to the Hall of Fame, he confided to *The Houston Chronicle* that he often wonders, "Did I really do that?"

The University of Houston star gets in the zone during practice before the 1983 NCAA semifinal against Louisville.

SHOT CALLER

Cheryl Miller
(b.1964)

One of Cheryl Miller's brothers (Darrell) caught for the California Angels and another (Reggie) starred for the Indiana Pacers. But she took a backseat to neither. The 6'2" multi-talented guard/forward scored a record-setting 105 points for Riverside (California) Polytechnic High School in a preposterous 179-15 win over Notre Vista (California) High. Her fierce competitiveness, athleticism, and ball-handling skills earned her three Naismith Player of the Year honors while at the University of Southern California, where she won back-to-back NCAA titles in 1983 and 1984. In 1995 Miller was inducted into the basketball Hall of Fame, daring little brother Reggie to follow in her footsteps.

Miller's Trojan teammates nicknamed her Silk for her smooth ball handing.

STEALTH BOMBER

Cynthia Cooper (b.1963)

When Cynthia Cooper retired from the WNBA the first time, her coach, Nancy Lieberman-Cline, went public to beg her to stay. No wonder. The scrappy guard led the Comets to four titles in the WNBA's first four seasons. With Jordan-esque charisma and an average of 21 points, 3.3 rebounds, and 4.9 assists a game, Cooper was the best clutch player in women's hoops. "Who else is going to take that [2000 championship game-tying] shot with 21 seconds left?" asked Lieberman-Cline. Cooper, who also won two NCAA titles at USC and an Olympic gold medal in 1988, finally listened to her coach's pleas in 2003. At 40, Cooper pulled another Jordan: She returned to the Comets, scoring 16 points per game before a season-ending shoulder injury. Coop became head coach at Prairie View A&M University, where she guided the women's basketball team to its first Southwestern Athletic Conference championships in 2007 and 2009. In 2010 she was enshrined in the Naismith Hall of Fame.

Spring-loaded Coop was the Comets' ultimate clutch shooter during their win against the Liberty in the 2000 Finals.

BIG FOOT

Shaquille O'Neal
(b.1972)

The man with the biggest feet
in the NBA (size 23, if you're
counting) has certainly left
a gargantuan footprint
on the NBA since getting
picked first overall in the
1992 draft by the Orlando
Magic. Unstoppable inside,
the 7'1" big man with four
championship rings leaves
defenders only one choice:
foul him to expose his
Achilles heel, free throws.

THE
MESSENGER

Dr. Edwin Bancroft Henderson (1883–1977)

Sure you can rattle off every name on the NBA's 50 Greatest Players list, but you better not forget the name Dr. Edwin Bancroft Henderson. He's the man responsible for taking hoops out of the classrooms of Harvard University and onto the playgrounds of black America.

The nation's first black instructor of physical education, Henderson graduated at the top of his class at Miner Normal School in 1904 and was accepted into a summer program for physical education at Harvard University. It was in Cambridge that Henderson first learned how to play the newly invented game of basketball.

Returning home to Washington, D.C., he set up basketball classes at the city's 12th Street YMCA. By 1906, he had organized six teams and set up championship games in D.C. and Brooklyn, New York. No benchwarmer

YMCA '09-'10

Sturlock Photo

Henderson, holding the
ball in front for his 1909–10

himself, Henderson suited up as a player/coach for D.C.'s legendary 12th Streeters. Colleges took notice of these new athletes: Members of Henderson's 1911 team went on to attend Howard University and star on that school's first collegiate basketball team.

Henderson's ambitions extended well beyond the court. In 1906 he led a group of educators to create the Inter-Scholastic Athletic Association (ISAA), the first amateur athletic conference for black high school and college athletes. And in 1910 Henderson led a successful campaign against the AAU to lift its ban on black athletes.

The doctor spent the rest of his life preaching the social benefits of sports by writing articles for white newspapers to publicize the talent of black athletes. Penning more than 3,000 letters to the editor to various newspapers, Henderson was also a constant contributor and avid supporter of the black press. His most notable work was *The Negro in Sports*, published in 1939—a chronicle that relied on the testimony of such pioneering black sportswriters as Wendell Smith of *The Pittsburgh Courier-Journal* and Sam Lacy and Art Carter of *The Baltimore Afro-American*.

In 1954, Henderson retired from D.C.'s public school system as the director of health and physical education for black schools, but he continued promoting the sport he loved so well. Four years before his death in 1977, he summed up his career: "Athletics has done more to bring Negroes in the mainstream of our American society than possibly any other medium." From Jim Crow to the civil rights movement, Henderson transformed the very nature of sports. And it would be only fitting if every fan, every Jordan, every city kid with a hoop dream, thanked him for the assist.

"Athletics has done more to bring Negroes in the mainstream of our American society than possibly any other medium."

—*Dr. Edwin Bancroft Henderson*

Henderson was accepted to Harvard's summer program in 1904, thanks in large part to the mentoring of Anita Turner, one of the nation's first black directors of physical culture.

BILL OF RIGHTS

Bill Russell (b.1934)

The first words that are usually used to describe Celtics legend Bill Russell today—dignified, tough, proud, self-sacrificing—are a far cry from the first words he heard from the white citizens of Monroe, Louisiana, in the late 1930s. Young William Russell watched as his parents, Charlie and Katie, were humiliated daily by whites. A gas station attendant once pulled a shotgun on Charlie when he objected to having to wait for all the white patrons to be served first. Finally fed up with the terrors of racism in the Deep South, the family packed up and settled in Oakland, California, in 1943.

Three years later, Russell's mother died from kidney failure. The 12-year-old Russell retreated into the world of books to escape the pain of his reality. During his pro career, his ingrained reliance on intellect and hard work

"My father once told me that anyone who worked for three dollars an hour owed it to himself to put in four dollars' worth of work so at the end of the day he could look any man in the eye and tell him where to go," the NBA great wrote in his autobiography, *Russell Rules*. "I rediscovered my father's words about the meaning of work, and I committed myself ... to making myself the best basketball player on the planet."

But early on, few would have tagged the gangly, introverted boy as a future NBA icon. Despite standing more than 6 feet tall by his teens, Russell showed no flashes of athletic greatness at McClymonds High School. If his coach, George Powles, had not decided to take him on as the 16th man on a 15-man squad,

A fierce rebounder, Russell also used every inch of his 6'9" frame to launch himself to the hoop, here breaching the Cincinnati Royals defense in 1958.

"I believe that man saved me from becoming a juvenile delinquent," the NBA star wrote in his first autobiography, *Go Up for Glory.* "If I hadn't had basketball, all my energies and frustrations would surely have been carried in some other direction." Still, Russell didn't start until his senior year of high school and was offered just one college basketball scholarship—to the University of San Francisco.

Russell exploded at USF and quickly became the most dominating center in college ball. With a precedent-setting lineup of three black starters—Russell, Hal Perry, and Russell's eventual Celtics teammate, K.C. Jones—the Dons won back-to-back NCAA championships and reeled off 60 consecutive wins.

On December 11, 1954, after a 47-40 loss to UCLA (USF's last before eventually winning 60 straight games), the *Los Angeles Times'* Jack Geyer gushed about Russell's performance. "In his all-round play, Russell was amazing. Time after time, he indulged in a sort of one-man volleyball, going high in the air to tap the ball over to where he would retrieve it unmolested." Some argue that Russell's dominating play was the catalyst for the NCAA goaltending rule.

Despite the growing respect for Russell's skills and the team's success, the stars were treated like second-class citizens. When USF headed to Oklahoma City for the All-College Tournament in 1955, the local hotel denied accommodations to Russell, Jones, and Perry, prompting the entire team to stay in empty dorms in protest.

Things did not get better for Russell when he joined the Boston Celtics in 1956. Incredibly, the Boston Garden rarely sold out during Russell's 13-season tenure—during which the Celts won 11 NBA titles. Teammate

"My father once told me that anyone who worked for three dollars an hour owed it to himself to put in four dollars' worth of work." —*Bill Russell*

Tom Heinsohn claimed that two white sportswriters in Boston told him they wouldn't vote for Russell as most valuable player because he was black. (Russell still won MVP five times.) White neighbors tried to prevent Russell from moving into their community and, when that failed, brutally harassed him.

Russell didn't shrink from these insults. He was one of the first celebrities to call himself black instead of Negro. And he was unrelenting in his fight for civil rights, joining the 1963 March on Washington and vocally supporting Muhammad Ali in his stance against the Vietnam War. When legendary Celtics coach Red Auerbach moved to the front office in 1966, he named the still active Russell as his replacement—the NBA's first black head coach.

As fiercely independent and stoic as Russell was during his career, he was the epitome of the team player. Personal stats, including out-scoring his friend and on-court rival, Wilt Chamberlain, were less important than team dynamics. "Star players have an enormous responsibility beyond their statistics," he wrote in his memoir, *Second Wind.* "I always thought that the most important measure of how good a game I'd played was how much better I'd made my teammates play."

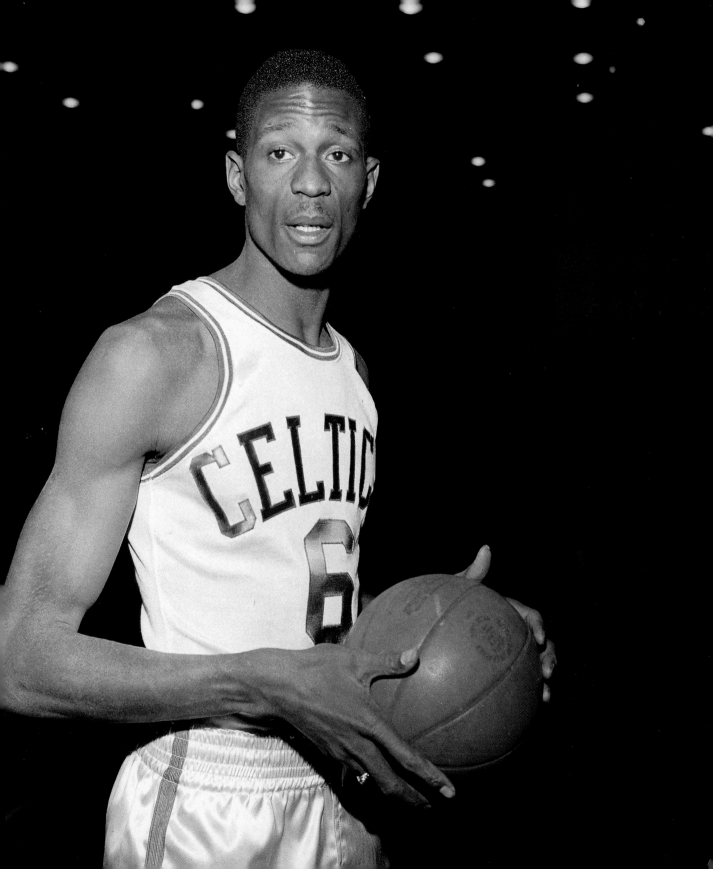

BASEBALL

➡ OUT OF THE PARK ⬅

Before Jackie and Doby crashed the gate, before Mays
could say "hey," the majors' exclusion of Negro Leaguers made
a sham out of America's Game.

Willie Mays
"Honest, I'm not swinging for
homers," Mays said before
this June 21, 1954, game
against the Cards. He then
hit his 19th and 20th four-
baggers of the season.

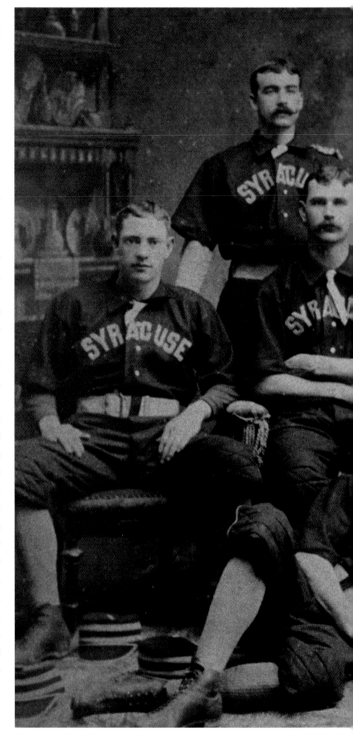

Walker (top row, far right) was shut out of the pro leagues when the Syracuse Stars folded in 1890.

REVERSAL OF FORTUNE

Moses Fleetwood Walker (1856–1924)

No one made much fuss over the color of Moses Fleetwood Walker's skin when he enrolled at Oberlin College in 1879. The school was a historically liberal institution, and Walker, who grew up in the abolitionist Quaker community of Mt. Pleasant, Ohio, was treated as just another bright, good-looking guy with a passion for baseball. Unfortunately, the rest of the world was far less enlightened, and Walker would suffer escalating racism throughout his life.

A superb catcher with charisma to spare, Walker was recruited by Cleveland's semi-pro White Sewing Machine team. He was shocked by the treatment he faced while traveling with the team. Hotels refused him, opponents wouldn't take the field against him, and crowds berated him. In 1883, Walker joined the Toledo Blue Stockings and became the first African-American in the majors when Toledo moved up to the American Association a year later—where even his teammates baited him. Pitcher Tony Mullane often refused to take signals from Walker, then tried to cross him up—his own catcher—with unexpected pitches. Despite his bullet arm, Fleet's pro career ended when his last AA team, the Syracuse Stars, folded in 1890. In 1908, the once optimistic baseball star wrote *Our Home Colony*, a book encouraging black Americans to give up the fight against racism in the U.S. and return to Africa.

THE WRITE STUFF

Sol White (1868–1955)

King Solomon White first fell in love with the fledgling national pastime at an unusual juncture in American history. Born in Reconstruction-Era Ohio, White and other African-American baseball greats regularly played on mostly white or mixed teams and leagues. That is, until the great white wall slammed down on black players for nearly a half century.

White broke in with the 1887 Pittsburgh Keystones of the National Colored League. But the league failed after a few weeks because the owners simply could not fill seats. White then joined the interracial Wheeling (West Virginia) Green Stockings as their starting third baseman and hit .381. Despite that gaudy average, his white teammates refused to play with him the next season. So he had to content himself with being the star infielder on some of the premier black teams of the age, including the 1891 world champion New York Gorhams, the Cuban Giants, and the Page Fence Giants. In 1895 he took a break from baseball to further his education at the historic all-black Wilberforce University.

In 1902 White joined forces with H. Walter Schlichter, a white sportswriter, to found the Philadelphia Giants, for whom he played shortstop and managed. White and his Philly teammates (including future Hall of Famers Rube Foster and Pop Lloyd) won four consecutive eastern championships, starting in 1904.

White was acutely aware that "separate but equal" meant black achievements would never be properly recognized. To protect black baseball from both white revisionism and obscurity, in 1907 he published *Sol White's History of Colored Baseball*.

After managing for several more years, White retired from baseball in 1926. He died before he was able to finance a second volume of his history, but in 2006, the contribution of black baseball's first chronicler was finally recognized when he was enshrined in the Hall of Fame.

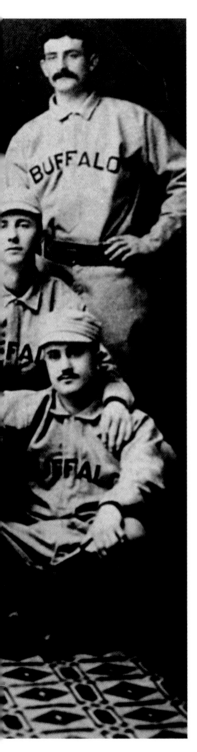

Grant, (bottom row, second from right) was the first black player to last three consecutive seasons on the same International League team. But in his final year with the Bisons, his team-mates refused to take a team photo with their best slugger.

BRUISED PEACH

John Henry "Pop" Lloyd (1884–1965))

After Ty Cobb's Detroit Tigers faced off against Pop Lloyd's Habana Reds in a 12-game exhibition series in 1910, Cobb claimed he would never play against a black man again. Why? Perhaps because Lloyd, one of the all-time great shortstops and sluggers, outsmarted the notorious Cobb. Knowing Cobb sharpened his cleats to shred infielders while he stole bases, Lloyd armored himself with iron shinguards. He also tagged out Cobb on three consecutive steal attempts. Or maybe Lloyd just bruised the super-slugger's ego. He out-batted Cobb .500 to .369 in that series.

THE DEPARTED

Frank Grant (1865–1937)

At 5'7" and weighing about a buck-fifty, Ulysses F. "Frank" Grant was small, but his accomplishments in the International League were huge. Considered one of the best second basemen of the 19th century, Grant was the first African-American to survive three consecutive seasons on a single team in the International League. It was no mean feat; despite his outstanding stats with the Buffalo Bisons from 1886 to 1888—in 1887 he hit .353 and led the IL with 11 homers—his white teammates didn't think he was good enough to be in the 1888 team photo. He was a constant target of taunts, even "Kill the nigger." In 1889, after his teammates threatened to boycott his presence, Grant walked away from the club and bounced around with several all-black teams, eventually becoming player-manager of the Cuban Giants in 1893. "I wish some of the people who watched him play were still around," said Marian Grant Royston, a relative. "Frank Grant must have loved the game to put up with everything he had to." After retiring at 38, he earned a living as a waiter, porter, and elevator operator.

KING OF THE HILL

Andrew "Rube" Foster (1879–1930)

Some say Andrew "Rube" Foster's untimely death in 1930 sealed the demise of the Negro National League, which occured the same year. Though he lived his last years in a mental institution, it was his sheer force of personality and spirit that seemed to keep the league he founded in 1920 afloat. While he was an active front-office executive, the man often called the "father of black baseball" was single-minded in pursuit of success for the NNL.

Soon after Foster joined the Waco Yellow Jackets in 1897, he earned the reputation as a killer on the mound with his fastball and unhittable fadeaway. Despite his success on championship squads like the Cuban X Giants and the Philadelphia Giants, Foster felt grossly undervalued. In 1907, as a player-manager of the Chicago Leland Giants, Foster negotiated an unprecedented percentage take of the team's gate proceeds. In 1910, he founded what would become the Chicago American Giants, a team that used strong pitching and a lineup of bunt-and-run specialists to win all but one championship from 1910 to 1922.

Not content to be at the mercy of white booking agents, Foster hosted the historic founding meeting for the Negro National League in February 1920. A shrewd executive, Foster retained control over his Chicago American Giants while acting as president of the NNL. Though he often maneuvered players for league parity, he was also accused of conflicts of interest, rigging schedules to favor his club and bullying other teams into trading their best talent. His own half-brother, Bill Foster, himself a future Hall of Famer, was unhappy when he was forced to leave the Memphis Red Sox to join his bossy older sibling's team. But the father of black baseball almost always got his way.

Kansas City Monarchs
(1920–1962)

The longest-running team in Negro baseball history, the Monarchs fielded some of the greats of the game, including "Cool Papa" Bell, Jackie Robinson, and Satchel Paige, and sent more of their players to the majors than any other team. The Monarchs (pictured here in 1936) barnstormed as an independent team after the first Negro National League folded in 1930. In 1937 they became charter members of the Negro American League.

➡

Next Page

Homestead Grays
(1912–1950)

During their 38-year history, the Homestead Grays honed their fierce game independently, free of the restrictions of league play. They finally joined the second iteration of the Negro National League in 1934, and with power slugger Buck Leonard (top row, far left), the Grays won nine consecutive NNL championships (1937-45) and three Negro League World Series titles.

Bell said that while his induction
into the Hall of Fame in 1974 was
an honor, his happiest moment
"was when they opened the door
in the majors to black players."

DIAMOND TOUGH

Oscar Charleston
(1896–1954)

Charleston, the barrel-chested Negro League great, battled umps, players, and owners with equal zeal. Lore has it that once, while traveling by train in 1935, Charleston ripped the hood off a Ku Klux Klansman who'd boarded to shout slurs at black riders. The outfielder backed up his bluster with stunning power on the diamond. In his 21 years playing for 13 teams, the Cobb-eqsue base-stealer amassed a batting average close to .350.

HOT FOOT

James "Cool Papa" Bell **(1903–1991)**

He ran the bags like a run-seeking missile, once circling the diamond in a reported 12 seconds. Satchel Paige liked to joke that his one-time teammate was so fast he could turn off a light switch and get under the bed covers before the room got dark. A notorious base bandit, he stole 175 bases in the 1933 season—though, to be fair, he did play some 200 games that year.

Bell was a perennial Negro League All-Star who sped the basepaths for more than 20 seasons with powerhouse clubs like the St. Louis Stars, the Homestead Grays, and the Pittsburgh Crawfords. Originally a tricky southpaw with a mean curveball and a fadeaway knuckler, Bell moved full-time to the outfield in 1924 with the Stars. His speed allowed him to play a shallow center, where he seemed to taunt batters. He also tormented pitchers, as evidenced by his .341 lifetime batting average.

By the time Jackie Robinson broke the color line, Bell was well into his 40s, but the majors wasted no time pursuing him. "I got letters from everybody, every team," he told the Associated Press. "I said, 'I'm through.' I broke every record there was and I still could hit, but my legs were gone. I used them up."

Manley didn't publicly correct the mistaken assumption that she was African-American until a 1973 interview.

COLOR BLIND

Effa Manley (1900–1981)

When Abe Manley, a one-time numbers runner and owner of the Newark Eagles, married the fetching Effa Brooks after meeting her at a 1932 World Series game, he had no clue that beauty was the least of her gifts. Manley was actually a white woman whose German-Asian-Indian mother remarried a black man after Effa was born. Manley, however, was not confused about her identity. Her heart belonged to the black community—and everyone thought the rest of her belonged there too. Despite her light skin, she would pass for black for most of her life.

"She was unique and effervescent and knowledgeable," Monte Irvin, an Eagles outfielder before he became a New York Giant in 1949, told MLB.com. "She ran the whole business end of the team." Co-owner of the Eagles, she also acted as one of the team's scouts, compiling some of the league's deepest rosters and signing future Hall of Famers Monte Irvin, Larry Doby, and Leon Day.

Manley's brains and beauty were matched only by her ferocity in the face of injustice. Outraged that Dodgers general manager Branch Rickey signed away Eagles pitching ace Don Newcombe in 1946, she fought a relentless campaign to get compensation for the Negro Leagues teams raided by MLB. Soon after, the Cleveland Indians caved to Manley's demands and paid the Eagles an unprecedented $15,000 for centerfielder Doby.

Though the Eagles closed shop in 1948, Manley's career was far from over. She just took her fight for civil rights to another venue, becoming the treasurer for the Newark chapter of the NAACP. In 2006 she became the first woman to be enshrined at Cooperstown.

KNOCKOUT

Willie Wells
(1905–1989)

Effa Manley's beauty was so mesmerizing, it is said to have led to a baseball first. The Eagles owner often used her wiles to signal to her players, crossing her shapely legs for a hit or run and uncrossing them for a bunt or steal. Lore has it that shortstop Wells was watching Manley's legs so intently while at bat that he was knocked cold by a pitch from Baltimore Elite Giant Bill Byrd. In his next game, Wells supposedly became the first professional baseball player to regularly wear protective headgear: He had to make do with a construction helmet.

THE BLACK BABE

Josh Gibson (1911–1947)

While official records in the Negro Leagues are sketchy, Josh Gibson may have pulled off what Babe Ruth never could. As the story goes, the Homestead Grays' 6'1" catcher knocked a 580-foot homer just a few feet short of the top of the centerfield wall at Yankee Stadium. Stolid and taciturn, Gibson was nonetheless a hugely popular draw on both the Grays and the Pittsburgh Crawfords, where he caught for Satchel Paige for five seasons.

After several years of health problems, Gibson was diagnosed with a brain tumor in 1943. Three months before Jackie cracked the bigs, Gibson died of a stroke at age 35. It was a tragic end to a supernatural career that included an estimated 962 homers in 17 years—248 more than the white Babe, dead himself the following year at 53.

Gibson, clearly safe at home, was called out during the 1944 East-West All-Star Negro Game.

New York Black Yankees

(1936–1948)

Co-owned by famed dancer Bill "Bojangles" Robinson, the New York Black Yankees fielded such greats as George Crowe, the Boston Braves' third black player. Here Black Yanks manager Tex Burnett (left) makes a point to infielder Harry Williams, pitcher Tom Parker, and outfielder Dan Wilson during a 1942 game.

Next Page

THE GODFATHER

Alejandro Pompez (1890–1974)

Alejandro Pompez could have been a character in a Martin Scorsese film. He was a hustler and one of the richest men in Harlem in the 1930s, raking in more than $8,000 a day in an illegal numbers operation. He was also one of the Negro Leagues' most influential and infamous owners as chief of the Cuban Giants.

The dapper Pompez grew up in Key West, Florida, before making his way to New York City in the 1920s, when he became the owner of the mixed-race Cuban Stars of the Eastern Colored League. After the Depression hit in 1929, Pompez shuttered the team. But by 1935, he was back in the game. He renamed his team the New York Cubans and joined the NNL. Dodging a grand jury indictment for his connection to the mob in the late 1930s, Pompez turned state's evidence against James Hines, a member of the Dutch Schultz crime family.

In 1947 the Cubans won both the NNL pennant and the World Series. But the astute Pompez, always one step ahead of trouble, knew that Jackie Robinson's leap to the majors meant the end of Negro Leagues baseball. The crafty owner negotiated a deal in which his Cuban Giants became a farm team for the major league New York Giants. He then convinced Giants owner Horace Stoneham to hire him as their top scout for Latin players throughout the Caribbean. Pompez' keen eye and negotiating skills helped him nab some of the majors' great Latin players, including Orlando Cepeda, Juan Marichal, and the Alou brothers: Matty, Jesus, and Felipe.

Pompez topped off his baseball career by serving on the committee to elect Negro Leaguers to the Hall of Fame, ushering in the likes of Satchel Paige, Josh Gibson, and, Cool Papa Bell. And in a special election in 2006, the man who once ruled the streets of Harlem was himself inducted into the Hall.

Indianapolis Clowns (1946–1988)

The Clowns were the Harlem Globetrotters of the diamond, combining comedic antics with damn good baseball. In this photo (circa 1954), manager Oscar Charleston puts his arms around King Tut, whose oversized glove was a giant crowd-pleaser, and Connie Morgan, the female second baseman. In 1952 the Clowns won the Negro American League with a young shortstop named Henry Aaron. After the club sold his contract to the Boston Braves, Aaron went on to hit 755 home runs in the major leagues. Even after their heyday, the Clowns had the last laugh.

In 1938, Pompez was a star witness at the conspiracy trial of James Hines, a major player in the Dutch Schultz crime family.

ON DECK

Larry Doby (1923–2003)

Following on the heels of Jackie Robinson by less than four months, Larry Doby had as rough a ride in the majors as Robinson, and without any of the glory— or the support system. As Willie Mays once pointed out, "Jackie had Pee Wee Reese and Gil Hodges and Ralph Branca, but Larry didn't have anybody." The Indians centerfielder—the first African-American in the American League and the second ever in MLB—was a lefthanded hitter who led the AL with 32 homers in 1952 and 1954. The seven-time All-Star won his World Series title in 1948, seven years before Robinson had his taste. Hall of Famer Joe Morgan said it best at Doby's memorial service in 2003: "Without guys like Larry Doby, the job Jackie Robinson started would not have been finished."

"It was 11 weeks between the time Jackie Robinson and I came into the majors," Doby once said. "Come on. Whatever happened to him happened to me."

LITTLE BOY BLUE

Roy Campanella (1921–1993)

Nobody who ever wore Dodger blue played with as much exuberance as Roy Campanella. The 5'9" sparkplug behind the plate never took for granted his salad years as one of the famed Boys of Summer from 1948 to 1957. It was too much fun. "You've got to be a man to play baseball for a living," said the eight-time All-Star. "But you've got to have a lot of little boy in you, too."

A brainy backstop with a rocket arm, Campanella also set the single-season record for catchers with 41 homers and a National League-best 142 RBIs in 1953. Campanella made a huge impact on the field—leading NL catchers in putouts six times and contributing to the Dodgers' five pennants—but it was the three-time NL MVP's unabashed bliss that still resonates 50 years later. "I never want to quit playing baseball," he once said. "They'll have to cut this uniform off of me to get me out of it."

On January 28, 1958, as he returned home from the Harlem liquor store he owned, Campanella broke his neck when his Chevrolet skidded off the road and overturned near his Long Island home. He eventually regained the use of his arms and hands, and never lost his vitality or his boyish enthusiasm for the game.

THE PAYBACK

Vic Power
(1927–2005)

Signed by the Yankees out
of Puerto Rico in 1951, Vic
Power should have been the
first person of color to wear
the pinstripes. That Power
didn't field well enough was
the Yanks' public excuse for
trading him. But he only went
on to win seven consecutive
Gold Gloves as the best-
fielding first baseman of his
time. Truth is, his showman-
ship and his unwillingness to
act humble left the Yankee
brass cold. Power's payback?
A 12-year career capped by
four All-Star appearances—
and, on May 19, 1961, a steal
of home for the Indians in
a come-from-behind win
against the Yankees.

IMAGINE THAT

Willie Mays (b.1931)

Is Willie Mays the best baseball player ever? Well, no sport lives by numbers more than baseball does. And the Say Hey Kid doesn't have the most homers. Or the highest batting average. Or the most stolen bases. Therefore the sum of the numbers says no. But perhaps no player has ever been better at as many aspects of the game.

Certainly there was no player more original. The basket catch, the flying hat—affectations, sure, but ones that sprinkled some much-needed color into a game that has had its share of gray conformists. The image of him flying into the gloom of the endless outfield of the old Polo Grounds to rob Cleveland's Vic Wertz of a game-changing hit in the 1954 World Series is one of baseball's best advertisements. And, according to Mays, it wasn't even one of his top two catches. Nah, says Willie, he caught not one but two balls bare-handed. For one of those, he had

to soar through the air so far that he knocked himself out when he landed.

The first player in the majors with 300 homers and 300 steals, Mays ran the bases with abandon, not just stealing them when everyone was looking, but taking the extra base when no one was. His arm? Well, that catch against Wertz is as well known for what followed: Mays somehow spinning into a reverse corkscrew and unleashing a strike back to the infield before most registered that he'd even caught the ball. And, of course, there was his bat; hampered by Candlestick Park's capricious winds, he still managed the fourth-best home run total ever, behind godson Barry Bonds, contemporary Hank Aaron, and Mr. Ruth.

You could say he was the first five-tool player ever, except he had a sixth tool that few in the game have come close to matching: imagination.

BRASS AND STEEL

Frank Robinson
(b.1935)

There's a moment that tells you all you need to know about Robinson, the first African-American to manage a major league team when he started directing the Indians in 1975. Eight years later, as the skipper of the Giants, he walked out to the mound to remove Jim Barr, his ineffectual reliever. Robinson got within a step of the mound when Barr flipped him the ball and started for the dugout. Robinson grabbed Barr by the shirt and tore into him. No I'm-just-glad-to-be-here shuffle for Frank Robinson. His spikes were sharpened from the moment he hit the majors, and they never dulled during his 50–year career from NL Rookie of the Year to league executive. Robby took no guff.

SWEET TALKER

Reggie Jackson
(b.1946)

With New York Yankees manager Billy Martin, Jackson shares a rare moment of tenderness after the Yanks' 8-4 win over the Dodgers in the 1977 World Series. Jackson earned his moniker Mr. October in that game with his unprecedented three consecutive homers. Add that feat to his career .490 slugging percentage and three slugging titles, and it's no wonder they named a candy bar after the guy. Said the loquacious outfielder, "After Jackie Robinson, the most important black in baseball history is Reggie Jackson. I really mean that."

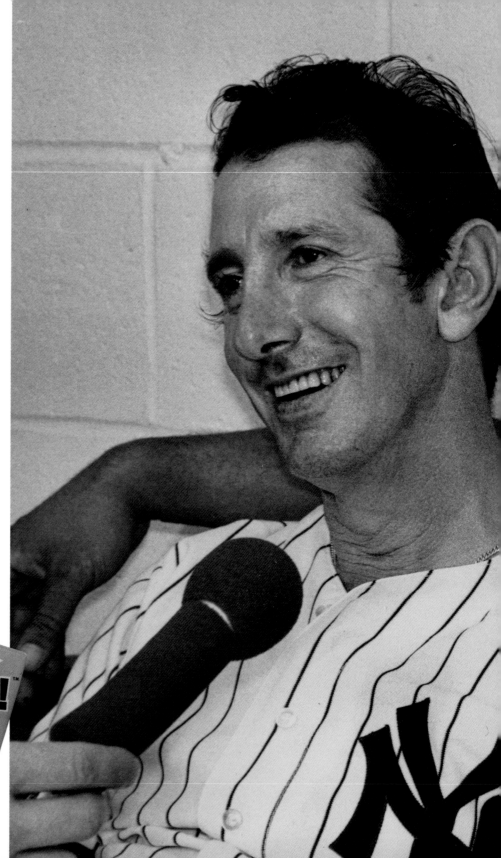

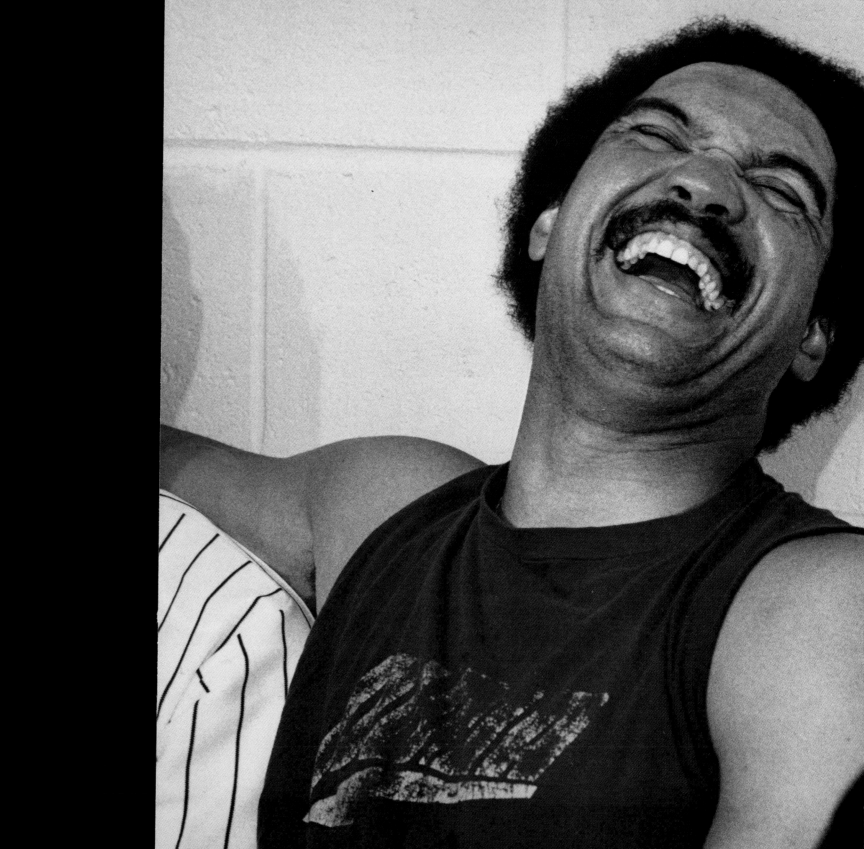

He may have been the oldest
rookie in Major League Baseball
history, but Paige was forever
young with his homespun wit.

THE KING
OF ZING

LeRoy "Satchel" Paige (c.1906–1982)

How good was Satchel Paige? Joe DiMaggio once called the lanky sharpshooter "the best and fastest pitcher I've ever faced." How durable was he? Try nearly 30 years of durability as a pro pitcher. His longevity makes a mockery of today's steroid-enhanced demigods. Chris Rock recently joked, "Satchel Paige led the league in ERA two years after he died." It's just the kind of crack that Paige, with a wit as sharp as his breaking ball, would have made.

While making his bones in the Negro Leagues for over 20 years, notably on the hallowed Pittsburgh Crawfords and the Kansas City Monarchs, the mighty righty honed a nearly preternatural intuition about hitters' soft spots. "When a batter swings and I see his knees move, I can tell just what his weaknesses are," he said. "Then I just put the ball where I know he can't hit it." He also had plenty of

time to finely tune his flair for a good show, which is no doubt why in 1935, Johnny Burton, a California promoter, offered Paige a chance to front his own team. "Satchel was really made for barnstorming," wrote teammate Frazier Robinson in his book, *Catching Dreams: My Life in the Negro Baseball Leagues.* "One time in Spokane, when I was catching for the [the Satchel Paige] All-Stars, he called in all three outfielders and moved them to the infield. Then he set the third baseman down on third base and the first baseman down on first base. Then he struck out the side."

Paige particularly enjoyed humiliating the Homestead Grays' home run king, Josh Gibson. As the story goes, Gibson once made the mistake of bragging that he would take Satch over the fence as Paige's family watched. In their next meeting, Paige walked the bases full with two

outs. Then he strolled from the mound to whisper to Gibson, "Here's your chance." Paige struck him out with two fastballs and a curve.

A year after Jackie Robinson broke into the majors, Bill Veeck, the Cleveland Indians owner, scoured the Negro Leagues desperate to find a star pitcher to get an edge in the pennant race. On July 7, 1948, Veeck tried out Paige, asking the pitcher to land five fastballs over a cigarette Veeck had placed on home base. When Paige nailed four, Veeck signed him on the spot for the remaining three months of the season. Two days later, on July 9, 1948, the roughly 42-year-old Paige became Major League Baseball's oldest rookie. By exactly how much, it's hard to say. "Age is a question of mind over matter," he famously said. "If you don't mind, it doesn't matter."

The St. Louis Browns didn't mind his age as much as the new pitch he unveiled in his first MLB outing, his "hesitation" pitch—which involved a slight pause, as his left foot hit the ground, before releasing the ball. Going 6-1 with a 2.48 ERA that season, Paige helped the Indians win the pennant by one game. In 1948, his hesitation pitch was ruled illegal.

The velocity of his arm was not matched by that of his legs. "I don't generally like running," he said. "I believe in training by rising gently up and down from the bench." In 1965, after a 12-year hiatus from the majors, the 59-year-old Paige returned to pitch for the Kansas City Athletics, becoming the oldest pitcher in an MLB game. Before the game, he hammed for the crowd, easing into a rocking chair and hiring a nurse to rub ointment on his arm.

Paige, who picked up his nickname as a kid carrying satchels at the Mobile, Alabama, railroad station, spent just six of his seasons in the majors, winning 28 games and losing 31 in 476 innings with 288 strikeouts and an ERA of 3.29—seemingly ordinary numbers that are astounding given his age. While Negro Leagues stats

"Age is a question of mind over matter. If you don't mind, it doesn't matter."

—Satchel Paige

Paige charmed everyone he met, from his first wife, Janet (with him below), to the gaggles of kids that regularly clamored for some playtime with their hero.

Paige shows off his pitching grip to his fellow 1952 American League All-Star teammates (from left) Mickey Mantle, Allie Reynolds, and Dom DiMaggio.

are unreliable, many historians believe Paige pitched a total of 2,500 games, 55 of them no-hitters, before an estimated 10 million people in the U.S., the Caribbean, and Central America. According to Paige, admittedly given to hyperbole, he won 104 of the 105 games he pitched in 1934 alone. In 1971, Paige became the first Hall of Fame inductee whose career had been spent mostly in the Negro leagues.

So what did he make of his role in integrating MLB? Paige had a typically incisive answer: "The only change is that baseball has turned Paige from a second-class citizen to a second-class immortal."

"I believe in training
by rising gently up and
down from the bench."

—*Satchel Paige*

THE FIRST

Jackie Robinson (1919–1972)

The bite-size version of Jackie Robinson's story is well chewed over: The Negro Leagues shortstop broke the color barrier in Major League Baseball when he stepped on the field with the Brooklyn Dodgers in 1947 and forever changed the game. He was named Rookie of the Year in 1947, led the NL in stolen bases in 1947 and 1949, was the NL MVP in 1949 and posted a .311 batting average over his 10-year career, during which the Dodgers won six pennants and one World Series. All of which he seemed to accomplish with a dazzling smile, an urbane wit, and a tolerance for abuse.

But Robinson was a man often at bitter odds with the America he loved. His goal was never to be the first beloved black superstar in the majors. ("I'm not concerned with your liking or disliking me ... all I ask is that you respect me as a human being," he once said.)

And his charm often masked his aggressive impatience and obsessive competitiveness.

Robinson was the youngest of five children raised by his sharecropper mother, Mallie, in Pasadena, California. Despite the daily assaults of discrimination, Mallie ingrained in her brood the belief that no one was superior to them. Robinson, a fiercely determined and intelligent kid, went on to win a scholarship to UCLA, where he was the school's first athlete to letter in track, basketball, baseball, and football in the same year. Even as an amateur athlete, Robinson had no tolerance for failure. "It kills me to lose. If I'm a trouble-maker—and I don't think that my temper makes me one—then it's because I can't stand losing. That's the way I am about winning; all I ever wanted to do was finish first," Robinson said.

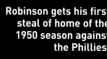
Robinson gets his first
steal of home of the
1950 season against
the Phillies.

"They better prepare to be rough, because I'm going to be rough with them."

—Jackie Robinson

Having scouted the Negro Leagues extensively, Dodgers general manager Branch Rickey felt that the Kansas City Monarchs' 26-year-old star had the mettle to withstand the immense pressures of integrating the majors. And he bet that Robinson's profile would be most easily digested by white America: a college educated second lieutenant in the Army, with a close family. But first, Rickey had a warning for Robinson: "Jackie, we've got no army. There's virtually nobody on our side. No owner, no umpires, very few newspapermen ... We can win only if we can convince the world that I am doing this because you're a great ballplayer and a fine gentleman."

Robinson, who once faced a court martial for protesting the treatment of blacks in the Army, would have to swallow his rage. Rickey made Robinson agree that for two years—no matter how brutally the fans jeered, no matter how many death threats he and his family received, no matter how times they raised the Confederate flag on the field—Jackie would not lash out. He would never present the image of an angry black man. And during that time, the famed Dodger was, at least in public, the epitome of grace under pressure, turning his cheek to the hate hurled at him, all the while tallying incredible stats for his team.

"I'm not concerned with your liking or disliking me ... all I ask is that you respect me as a human being."

—Jackie Robinson

But by his third year, Robinson had enough of the taunts and the pitches to his head. "They better prepare to be rough, because I'm going to be rough with them," Robinson reportedly said at the start of the 1949 season. His teammate Carl Erskine saw firsthand that no matter how popular he became, Robinson was still considered a second-class citizen. "By 1949, America embraced Jackie Robinson as its next superstar," wrote Erskine in his book *What I Learned from Jackie Robinson: A Teammate's Reflections On and Off the Field*. "But what television viewers ... might not have realized was that when the camera lights were turned off ... he was still treated as a black man first and a man second. And this broke Jackie's heart on a daily basis." And it galvanized him. For the previous two years, for example, Robinson agreed to avoid the Chase Hotel in St. Louis where his white teammates stayed. But in 1949, he demanded a room—and got it. (Still, even five years later, the hotel wouldn't serve Robinson or any of the black players in the dining room.)

On the field, Robinson was even more ferocious. Here's what Willie Mays said about Jackie's game: "The greatest catch I ever made was in Ebbets Field in Brooklyn, back in '51. I ran so far and dove so hard, I knocked myself out when I caught the ball. When I woke up, there were two people staring down at me: Leo [Durocher, manager of the New York Giants] and Jackie. I looked up at Jackie and said, 'What are you doin' here, Jackie?' And Jackie said, 'I just wanted to make sure you had the damn ball.'" The kicker? Traded to the Giants in 1957 as his skills declined, Robinson retired rather than play for a team he'd grown to despise.

His toughness and laser-like focus were natural fits for the business world during his post-baseball years. He was named director of personnel for coffee manufacturer Chock Full o'Nuts and later chairman of Freedom National Bank in Harlem. And he finally could devote more of his time to being an ardent civil rights activist, serving on the boards of the NAACP and the Congress of Racial Equality, leading rallies for Dr. Martin Luther King Jr., and debating race in America with Malcolm X.

Still, in his 1972 autobiography *I Never Had It Made*, Robinson expressed enormous disappointment that America had not lived up to its promise of equality for all. "I cannot stand and sing the anthem. I cannot salute the flag. I know that I am a black man in a white world."

As a family man, Robinson, pictured with wife Rachel and son Jackie Jr., was an appealing icon for white America.

BOXING

➡ **FIGHT FOR JUSTICE** ⬅

Without the stings of Jack Johnson, Sam Langford, Joe Louis, and Sugar Ray Robinson, The Greatest could never have floated above the sweet science.

Muhammad Ali
While training for his 1971 bout against the undefeated Joe Frazier, Ali was still shaking off ring rust from his long exile from boxing for his refusal to fight in the Vietnam War.

PRIDE AND PREJUDICE

Sam Langford (c.1883-1956)

Heavyweight champ Jack Johnson was five years older and about 40 pounds heavier than Sam Langford when the men first fought. And despite the 15-round pounding Langford took that day in 1906—or perhaps because of it—he earned Johnson's lifelong respect. "I put Langford to the mat for a count twice—the first with a right to the heart, the second an upper cut to the chin," said Johnson. "It was a wonder that he could stand the beating." At 5'6", Langford had a massive torso and long arms. But it was his uncanny ability to dole out—and withstand—the worst pummelings that earned him the nickname The Boston Terror.

Langford learned to take a beating at the hands of his father, who brutally abused his son. At 12 years old, Langford fled his Nova Scotia, Canada, home for Boston, where he swept up at a local gym and sparred with older, much stronger men. Langford seemed impervious to pain—and oblivious to his own limitations. The diminutive boxer fought in several weight classes in his 23-year career, clawing his way to an estimated 164–35–33 record with 115 knockouts, drubbing the likes of lightweight champ Joe Gans, lightweight Jack Blackburn, and heavyweight Joe Jeannette.

Johnson refused to fight Langford again after the 1906 match, saying, "I found [Langford] one of the toughest adversaries I ever met in the ring." Langford was forced to retire in 1926, when he wandered to the wrong corner during a fight. It turned out he'd been boxing almost totally blind in his left eye for nearly a decade.

STAR POWER

Sugar Ray Robinson (1921-1989)

Long before George Foreman hawked his first grill on QVC, Ray Robinson was raking in the dough with an assortment of successful Harlem businesses: Sugar Ray's Restaurant, Golden Gloves Barber Shop, and Edna Mae's Lingerie Shop. He was also the first sports star to understand his charisma was worth top dollar, literally tap-dancing for $15,000 a week at big venues.

Although many boxers have followed his lead in monetizing their fame outside of the ring, he was inimitable in it. During his pro career from 1940 to 1965, Robinson (born Walker Smith Jr.) racked up an astounding 202 fights—more than Joe Louis and Muhammad Ali combined. He held the world welterweight title for five years and the world middleweight title five times—never once falling to a 10-count, and suffering just a single TKO.

Jack "The Raging Bull" LaMotta was obsessed with beating Robinson, who defeated him in five of their six bouts. Robinson's power was legendary. In the lowest moment of his career, he accidentally killed boxer Jimmy Doyle in the ring; Doyle never regained consciousness after Robinson knocked him out in their 1947 contest. But Robinson was more than brute force. According to ring announcer Don Dunphy, "He could punch, he could take a punch, and he was as game as they come ... Any ingredient that any champion ever had, he had them all."

Dunphy isn't alone in his admiration for the man Ali called "the king, the master, my idol." Sugar Ray Leonard said of his namesake, "Believe me, there's no comparison [between us]. Sugar Ray Robinson was the greatest."

Retaking the middleweight crown on March 25, 1958, Robinson lands a crushing right to Carmen Basilio.

POLAR OPPOSITES

Floyd Patterson (1935–2006) and Muhammad Ali (b.1942)

In a relaxed moment that belied the enormous tension between Patterson and Ali, the former champ and the current one announced their upcoming fight in 1965. Patterson, who had become the youngest heavyweight champ in 1956 and the first champ to regain his title in 1960, was embraced by the sports establishment and was an ardent integrationist. Ali, who represented Black Nationalism and had recently shed his birth name Cassius Clay, called Patterson an Uncle Tom and "the technicolor white hope" for refusing to call him by his adopted moniker. And Ali went further: "I'm going to put him flat on his back so that he will start acting black." Patterson was sorely overmatched in the fight. But rather than going for a quick KO, Ali toyed with Patterson, pulling punches before finally putting him to the mat in the 12th round. Years later, Ali, who once dismissively nicknamed Patterson The Rabbit for his quick hands, would call him the most skilled boxer he ever fought.

LORDS OF
THE RING

Joe Frazier
(b.1944) and
Muhammad Ali
(b.1942)

On December 30, 1970, Frazier
(left) and Ali ignited one of the
most hyped rivalries in sports
at their contract signing for
the "Fight of the Century."
Ali may have won the verbal
fracas that afternoon, but on
March 8, 1971, the undefeated
Frazier had the upper hand.
"He wasn't The Greatest,
and he certainly wasn't THEE
Greatest," Frazier wrote in his
autobiography. "It became my
mission to show him the error
of his foolish pride. Beat it into
him." Frazier did more than
wound Ali's pride in that fight.
After he knocked Ali down with
a ferocious left hook in the
15th round, Smokin' Joe won a
unanimous decision, giving
The Greatest the first loss of
his pro career.

BREAKING ALL THE RULES

Jack Johnson (1878-1946)

Jack Johnson may very well have been be the world's first rock star. He was deadly in the ring, iconoclastic out of it, and his example, which reverberates still in the culture, changed the way African-Americans viewed themselves.

Jazz great Miles Davis wrote in the liner notes of his 1970 album, *A Tribute to Jack Johnson*, "Johnson portrayed freedom—it rang just as loud as the bell proclaiming him champion. He was a fast-living man. He liked women—lots of them and most of them white ... He smoked cigars, drank only the best champagne, and prized a seven-foot base fiddle on which he'd proudly thump jazz. His flamboyance was more than obvious. And no doubt mighty whitey felt 'no black man should have all this.'"

Johnson embodied the rage, the pride, and the thirst for justice that many blacks felt then—and now. Nearly 38 years after Davis published the elegy, Sean "Diddy" Combs echoed the sentiment in an interview with *The Source* magazine. "I'm the return of Jack Johnson. His whole swagger, personality, the way he whupped yo ass, it's the dress, the style, the cars, and the money ... This man would rent whole trains, get six or seven women, take them away for six months and rent out the top floor of hotels [at] a time when they were lynching niggas." Johnson would no doubt love that these wild, often apocryphal tales of debauchery are still alive and kicking butt.

The more he lashed out against those who wanted to keep him in his place, the more he captivated the nation— and scandalized white America. Not least because of his terrifying skills in the ring. "Johnson boxed on his toes, could block from most any angle, was lightning fast

> "The Jack Johnson–Jim Jeffries fight in 1910 was the most awaited event in black-American history."
>
> —*Arthur Ashe*

Jeffries was coaxed out of a five-year retirement to take on Johnson in the original "Fight of the Century."

SAN FR

CONTESTANT

JAMES J. JEFF

	35 YRS.	REACH	75 I
HT	6 FEET 1½ IN.	WAIST	38
	18 "	THIGH	26
NORMAL	45 "	CALF	17
EXPANDED	50 "	ANKLE	10

CHRONICLE HAS

on his feet, could feint an opponent into knots," wrote *Ring Magazine* founder Nat Fleischer in his book *Black Dynamite*. "[He] possessed everything a champion could hope for: punch, speed, brains, cleverness, boxing ability, and sharp-shooting."

The fifth-grade dropout from Galveston, Texas, made a living with his hands even before he stepped into the ring, working as a porter and carriage painter. The pay wasn't any better when he started his boxing career: He won $1.50 for his first professional fight. "There was nothing more for me to do in Galveston," Johnson said later, "If I stayed there, all I'd have is debts."

Johnson landed in Springfield, Illinois, in an 1899 match that was part slave auction, part circus act: Seven or eight black, blindfolded boxers would bloody each other in this "Battle Royale" while white spectators tossed change into the ring. Johnson duked it out until he was the last man standing. Jack Curley, assistant to boxing promoter P.J. "Paddy" Carroll, was stunned by Johnson's boxing talent and took the ornery fledgling under his wing.

By 1901, Johnson hit his biggest payday to date when he avenged his 1899 loss to black boxer John "Klondike" Haines in Memphis for a $1,000 purse—much less than he

PHOTOGRAPHS TAKEN BY THE CHRONICLE STAFF PHOTOGRAPHER, A. S. JOHNSON,
IMMEDIATELY AFTER ARRIVAL OF FIGHTERS IN CALIFORNIA
TO COMMENCE TRAINING

JACK JOHNSON

		AGE	32 YRS.	REACH	72 IN.		
EPS	16 IN.	HEIGHT	6 FEET 1 IN.	WAIST	36 "	BICEPS	16 IN.
EARM	13 "	NECK	17 "	THIGH	23 "	FOREARM	14 "
IST	8½ "	CHEST NORMAL	39 "	CALF	15 "	WRIST	10½ "
IGHT	128 LBS.	CHEST EXPANDED	42 "	ANKLE	9½ "	WEIGHT	212 LBS.

…would have earned fighting white boxers of equal caliber. But mixed-race bouts were illegal in most southern states. Johnson, however, was not a man deterred by the law, especially a racist law. Daring to fight white boxer Joe Choynski in Galveston landed both boxers in jail for 23 days, ostensibly for staging an unregulated contest. While incarcerated, the two sparred for the inmates and staff, drawing huge crowds.

Johnson eventually settled in California and by 1903, was the unofficial Negro heavyweight champion of the world. But busting up black contenders like Sam McVey, Joe Jeannette, and Sam Langford wasn't enough for Johnson. He was intent on being the best in the world. James J. Jeffries, the reigning champion in 1903, however, refused to fight a "colored" man and retired in 1905 undefeated. Finally, in 1908, Tommy Burns, the reigning world heavyweight champion, agreed to fight Johnson on December 26, in Australia, for $30,000.

"I'll beat the nigger or my name isn't Tommy Burns," promised the boxer whose real name was actually Noah Brusso. Before a shocked crowd of about 20,000 people, Johnson easily defeated Burns to become the world's first black heavyweight champion. His take for winning was only $5,000. As "white hope" after "white hope" failed to dethrone the flashy Johnson, the boxer flaunted his dominance. Johnson had an insatiable desire for white women at a time when just looking at one was cause for a lynching. Johnson sported furs and gold teeth nearly a century before the hip-hop generation was born.

Desperate white fans, including *The Call of the Wild* author Jack London, pressed Jeffries to come out of retirement to, as London wrote, "Remove the golden smile

Jeffries entered the ring for "The Fight of the Century" on July 4, 1910, in Reno, Nevada.

"The Jack Johnson-Jim Jeffries fight in 1910 was the most awaited event in black-American history," Arthur Ashe told *Sports Illustrated* in 1997. "It took months for word of the Emancipation Proclamation to circulate through the land, but 80% of black America knew of that fight." Black churches prayed for Johnson's victory. Black newspapers touted his battle against racism. Some black folks mortgaged their homes to bet on Johnson.

The press feared the worst. "If the Negro loses, the members of his race will be taunted and irritated because of their champion's downfall," predicted *The New York Times*. Johnson did little to allay anxieties. "Jeffries can't touch me," the boxer boasted days before the historic clash. Jeffries did manage to split Johnson's lip, but was badly overmatched. Johnson knocked out Jeffries in the 15th round. "I could never have whipped Johnson at my best," Jeffries said. "I couldn't have hit him. No, I couldn't have reached him in 1,000 years."

Johnson's hard-partying lifestyle and nose-thumbing at the law finally caught up with him in 1913. He was charged under the Mann Act for traveling across state lines with a white prostitute named Belle Schreiber. He fled the country with his second white wife, Lucille Cameron. But his career floundered abroad and Johnson returned to the States in 1920 to serve his jail time.

By the time he was released, Johnson was past his prime, though he continued to stage exhibitions in Europe. On June 10, 1946, Johnson died while crashing one of his flashy cars into a pole. No doubt, the bigger-than-life, hard-partying Johnson would have much preferred to go

Two months after
loss of his pro ca
Max Schmeling in Jur
Louis was already p
to take back h

AMERICAN
CLASSIC

Louis (1914–1981)

ouis never had to struggle to earn a living in the
By the time he picked up the sport in 1931, Jack
son had already KO'd the racial barrier. Earning
rom white America, however, was a bigger battle.
y though, his grace and dignity won over even the
callous of boxing fans. Eventually, Louis became
ining example of the Greatest Generation.

is, the second black world heavyweight champ and
f the country's first sports superstars, paved the way
frican-American athletes in America. "Joe made it
or me and other fellows now in baseball," Jackie
son once said. "I'm sure his example had a lot to
th my breaking in big-league ball. I imagine that
gers general manager] Mr. Rickey said to himself
considering the idea 'Joe Louis has proven that a

Negro can take honors and remain dignified. If we
like that in baseball, the job won't be hard.'"

Born Joe Louis Barrow, the icon had to learn
a punch early. Being the seventh of eight childr
growing up in Chambers County, Alabama, wa
enough. But in 1916, when Louis was 2 years c
father, Munroe, was committed to an asylum. Eve
eight mouths to feed, his mother, Lillie, didn't cra
eventually married again to Patrick Brooks, who ha
kids of his own. The family left the South in the mid
and headed for Detroit.

Hunger was Joe's first impulse when he was lu
boxing, the sport *du jour* in the Motor City. When h
that boxers at Brewster Center Gym got paid in f
entered his first fight—a loss, but he won $7 in gr

Pvt. Joe Louis says_

"We're going to do our part
... and we'll win because
we're on God's side"

Louis became the embodiment
of American patriotism (left)
after he knocked out Nazi
hope Max Schmeling in just
over two minutes of their
1938 rematch (right).

Louis didn't fight again until 1931, when he spent the 50 cents his mother had given him for violin lessons to rent out a locker at the local gym. According to legend, when his name wouldn't fit on his amateur boxing uniform, he dropped his last name and became Joe Louis.

By the time he turned pro in 1934, he'd won all but four of his amateur fights and the AAU light heavyweight national championship. Three years later, Louis was the number one contender in the heavyweight division. His managers, Julian Black and John Roxborough, counted on the white judges discriminating against Louis, so they had trainer Jack Blackburn teach the fighter to leave no doubt about the winner: He became the KO king and the Brown Bomber was born. Black, Roxborough, and Blackburn also made sure that Louis was as appealing to whites as Jack Johnson was resolutely terrifying to them. The trio's tutoring in PR-perfect charm and low-key living made Joe Louis a palatable product. And America ate it up.

After 27 straight wins, including 23 KOs, Louis suffered his first professional loss in 1936 when German Max Schmeling knocked him out in the 12th round before a crowd of 60,000 at New York's Yankee Stadium. But the bruiser rallied and went on to win the world heavyweight crown in 1937 after he KO'd James J. Braddock in the eighth round at Chicago's Comiskey Park.

Detroit's adopted son held the heavyweight crown from 1937 to 1948 and successfully defended it 25 times, a

division record. Of his many memorable wins, however, his rematch with Schmeling in June 1938 was the highlight. Schmeling was literally the poster boy for Hitler's Aryan Nation. Like Jesse Owens had two years earlier at the 1936 Olympics, a black man would be representing all Americans, not just black Americans. With the U.S. on the precipice of World War II, President Franklin D. Roosevelt met with Louis the night before the fight to lend support: "Joe, we need muscles like yours to beat Germany." Louis knocked out Schmeling in just over two minutes into the first round. The Brown Bomber became the embodiment of American patriotism.

Taking FDR's cue to heart and at the height of his career, Louis enlisted in the Army in 1942, where he served until 1945. In addition to fighting in exhibition matches for GIs in the States, North Africa, and Europe, Louis also took up the fight against racism in the armed forces, refusing to box before segregated crowds. And after Jackie Robinson and other black soldiers were denied entry to officer candidate school, Louis successfully campaigned to get them admitted.

His tireless civil rights work continued after he retired from boxing. An avid golfer, Louis didn't just fund pioneering golfers like Teddy Rhodes, who also coached Louis; he blazed his own trails on the links too. His entry into the San Diego Open in 1952 attracted much-needed attention to the PGA's whites-only policy. Though the PGA denied entry to Bill Spiller and Rhodes

"Joe, we need muscles like yours to beat Germany."

—President Franklin D. Roosevelt

"I'm sure his example had a lot to do with my breaking in big league ball."

—Jackie Robinson

that year, the organization could not stand the embarrassment of denying entry to one of the nation's most beloved figures.

Martin Luther King Jr. often recounted the story of the young black prisoner whose dying words in the gas chamber were, "Save me, Joe Louis. Save me, Joe Louis." The boxer heard many pleas in his life and was generous to a fault. He said he never regretted giving his money away, even when the IRS hounded him for half a million dollars in back taxes. Unable to pay his debt, he was reduced to working as a greeter at Caesar's Palace in Las Vegas just to make ends meet.

Sadly, the man with a heart of gold was plagued by heart problems later in life. His friend Frank Sinatra paid for two heart operations, but the Bomber ultimately died of a heart attack on April 12, 1981, in Las Vegas. At the behest of President Ronald Reagan, Joe Louis was buried in Arlington National Cemetery with full military honors.

Despite being knocked down twice by Joe Walcott (right) in his last title defense in December of 1947, the Brown Bomber was still able to hold on to the heavyweight crown.

TENNIS

➡ **BLACKS IN WHITES** ⬅

The Williams sisters are heirs to a long line of African-

American players who have been breaking serves since

Lucy Diggs Slowe first picked up a racket.

Serena Williams
**Showing her championship
form, Williams hits a return
against Justine Henin in the
final of the 2010 Australian
Open—the 12th Grand Slam
title of a career that's still
going strong.**

Slowe is pictured here
circa 1917, the year she
became the first American
Tennis Association women's
singles champion.

SMASH HIT

Lucy Diggs Slowe (1885–1937)

The mother of black tennis, Lucy Diggs Slowe, could be punishing on the court. But off it, she committed her life to nurturing the black community, paving the way for champions like Jimmie McDaniel, Althea Gibson, Arthur Ashe, Lori McNeil, and Zina Garrison. The United States Lawn Tennis Association did not admit African-Americans (and wouldn't until 1948), so in 1916 Slowe and other black athletes helped form the American Tennis Association. Fittingly, Slowe won the singles title at the first ATA National Championship at Baltimore's Druid Hill Park Tennis Courts in 1917.

Slowe's accomplishments extended far beyond the court. While attending Howard University, she was the first president of Alpha Kappa Alpha sorority. After graduating as valedictorian in 1908, she taught English and went on to earn a master's degree from Columbia in 1915. Seven years later, Slowe was appointed the first Dean of Women at Howard University.

But her true legacy began in 1935 when Slowe was handpicked to join 28 of the nation's top African-American female leaders to work with Mary McLeod Bethune, who was a special advisor on minority affairs to President Franklin D. Roosevelt. Their goal: to establish the National Council of Negro Women, a group formed to lead, develop, and advocate for black women and their families. Today, the NCNW reaches some 4 million women. History proves that Lucy Diggs Slowe, like any good mother, led by example.

Johnson (right, with Arthur Ashe) planted the seeds for the integration of a whites-only sport.

DOCTOR LOVE

Robert "Whirlwind" Johnson (1899–1971)

The name Dr. Robert Walter "Whirlwind" Johnson doesn't mean much to most tennis fans. But without him, we may have never known Althea Gibson and Arthur Ashe.

The doctor, whose medical clinic in Lynchburg, Virginia, was the first minority-owned practice in the city, had become a rabid tennis fan during his residency at Prairie View Hospital in Prairie View, Texas. He became so enamored of the game that he opened an ad hoc tennis camp on the grounds of his home. Before long, an unofficial black tennis development program took shape.

Johnson began scouting the nation for the best black players. After seeing Althea Gibson at an ATA tournament in 1946, he signed her on the spot. He would do the same with a young Arthur Ashe eight years later. In the early 1950s, he prevailed upon Edmund Penzold, director of the USLTA National Interscholastic Championships, to invite blacks. The first integrated event was a disappointment, though: his two best players, Victor Miller and Roosevelt Megginson, lost in the first round.

That did not deter Johnson. Decades before Nick Bollettieri opened his eponymous tennis academy, Johnson created the ATA Junior Development Program. Using his own funds, the father of black tennis housed, coached, and taught the nation's top African-Americans to use their talent and education to fight racism.

NET LOSS

Jimmie McDaniel (c.1917–unknown)

Not just a game for country folk, tennis caught on in urban areas when African-Americans like McDaniel (right) began hitting the courts. A perennial tennis champ out of Xavier University, McDaniel was a regular at the Cosmopolitan Tennis Club in New York City (here in 1940). Though McDaniel was a big attraction on the ATA tour, winning the men's singles title in 1939, '40, '41, and '46, he retreated into relative obscurity along with the other players on the black tennis circuit. But as late as 1979, McDaniel was still teaching tennis to youngsters.

Serena (left) and Venus Williams
prepare to take on Rika Hiraki and
Kirstin Freye in the first round
of the 2002 Wimbledon doubles
championship. The sisters would
ultimately take home the title.

DYNAMIC DUO

Venus Williams (b.1980) and Serena Williams (b.1981)

Tough-love tennis dad Richard Williams never doubted his girls Venus and Serena were born to win. As boldly as Althea Gibson 50 years earlier, the cornrowed Williams sisters from Compton, California, crashed onto the tennis scene in the late '90s and stunned competitors with their pure power and grace.

With her sizzling serve, Serena defeated defending champ Martina Hingis in a second-set tiebreaker to win the U.S. Open in 1999, her first Grand Slam title. The next year, Venus won both Wimbledon and the U.S. Open, the first black woman to hold both titles since Gibson in 1958. Venus defended her titles in 2001 and was on her way to a three-peat until little sis came along and snatched the two trophies in 2002, beating Venus in the finals both times.

Big, black, and proud, the Williams sisters ramped up the intensity of the competition and brought a whole new wave of attention to the sport. The young women made history at the 2000 Olympics, when Venus took the gold in singles, a first for a black woman. Then she and Serena topped it off with a doubles gold.

Their faceoff at the 2001 U.S. Open was the first women's tennis final aired on prime-time television. Starting with the 2002 French Open, the siblings made an unprecedented run during which they met up in the finals of four consecutive Grand Slam tournaments. "Every day they are active and visible in tennis, the sport is stronger," said tennis icon Billie Jean King. Madison Avenue has certainly taken advantage of the media frenzy, rewarding the young women with huge endorsement contracts. In 2004 *Forbes* magazine ranked the women—Serena at $9.5 million and Venus at $8.5 million—as the highest-paid female athletes.

Even with all their wealth, fame, and adulation, the Williams sisters still recognize that they have reaped a hard-won harvest sowed by others. "I have all the opportunities today because of people like Althea," Venus said at the 2007 ceremony honoring the 50th anniversary of Gibson's win at the U.S. Open. "I'm just trying to follow in her footsteps."

Though Serena (left) would eventually have to pull out of the 2007 Wimbledon doubles championship due to a calf injury, she and Venus soundly beat Claire Curran and Anne Keothavong in the first round, 6-1, 6-3.

AN UNLIKELY CHAMPION

Althea Gibson (1927-2003)

Long before bad girls were cool, two-time Wimbledon champion Althea Gibson broke all the rules. As a teenager, her penchant for skipping school and partying in Harlem's pool halls unnerved her parents, who had only recently come North for a better life, along with millions of other blacks during the Great Migration.

Born in Silver, South Carolina, Gibson and her family moved to Harlem when Althea was 3. The family of seven, once dirt-poor, was now city-poor, crammed in a tiny apartment uptown. Stifled, Gibson escaped to the streets, where she excelled in sports. "I just wanted to play, play, play," said the self-proclaimed "Harlem street rebel."

Paddle tennis launched Gibson's career. Her reputation for crushing anyone who dared to step on the mini-tennis court drew the attention of bandleader Buddy Walker, who figured court tennis might challenge the headstrong Gibson. She took immediately to the bigger court, where the intensity of her game gained her entry into the Cosmopolitan Tennis Club in Harlem's posh Sugar Hill section. It was here that elite black tennis players honed their skills. Club members were so awed by Gibson's power and athleticism that they sponsored her junior club membership. And after just one year of training, Gibson won the junior championship of the all-black American Tennis Association.

In 1946, Gibson's life changed forever when she met Dr. Whirlwind Johnson, a tennis enthusiast and unofficial talent scout for the ATA. Johnson, who would later recruit and coach Arthur Ashe, was looking for a prodigy to break the color barrier. He recognized Gibson's raw talent but

saw she needed grooming both on and off the court. With the permission of Gibson's frustrated parents, the doctor became Gibson's tennis guru and recruited fellow tennis enthusiast and civil rights activist Dr. Hubert Eaton as her guardian. Eaton made sure Gibson got the education and social training she'd need to win a college scholarship. Eaton's wife, Celeste, taught the etiquette-averse Gibson proper manners and style.

Thanks to Johnson's mentoring, Gibson won a scholarship to Florida A&M University and 10 consecutive ATA national titles. The tennis prodigy was ready to break the color line, but she needed help. Luckily, Gibson had won friends in high places.

In 1950, Alice Marble, the 1939 Wimbledon champ, wrote a scathing editorial in *American Lawn Tennis*, the official USLTA magazine, criticizing the organization for denying Gibson entry into the whites-only league. The article attracted national attention and soon after, the Orange Lawn Tennis Club in South Orange, New Jersey, invited Gibson to play in the USLTA's Eastern Grass Court Championships in August of that year.

The first person to integrate the USLTA, Gibson advanced history in South Orange that day. But almost as important to the super-competitive Gibson, she also advanced to a historic match against the Wimbledon singles champion, Louise Brough, four weeks later. Many argue that had it not been for a thunderstorm in Forest Hills, Gibson would have won that day. She was up 7-6 in the third set when play was suspended; Bough rebounded the next day to win.

"If your first serve ain't good, I'll knock it down your throat."

—*Althea Gibson*

Gibson had proven she was a world-class player. [In]
1951, the USLTA invited her to Wimbledon. Africa[n]
Americans everywhere took pride in Gibson's feat, an[d]
many supported her career financially. Boxers Joe Lou[is]
and Gibson's longtime friend Sugar Ray Robinson raise[d]
money for her travels abroad.

In her first Wimbledon appearance, Gibson lost in th[e]
third round to Beverly Baker of Santa Monica, Californi[a,]
6-1, 6-3. No matter. Gibson returned home a hero, eve[n]
more determined to sharpen her skills. She continued t[o]
study the game and compete in formerly all-white tourna[-]
ments, slowly climbing the USLTA rankings.

Gibson won the 1956 French Open, but the true tes[t]
was Wimbledon, and by 1957, she was ready mentall[y]
and physically. "I was ruthless on the tennis court," sh[e]
said of the 1957 Wimbledon. "Win at any cost. I becam[e]
an attacker. If your first serve ain't good, I'll knoc[k]
it down your throat." The young woman who seeme[d]
doomed to a troubled life won her first of two straigh[t]
Wimbledon championships and was welcomed home t[o]
a ticker-tape parade.

After winning five Grand Slam singles titles, Gibso[n]
tried singing, acting, and golf—as the first black player o[n]
the LPGA tour, she was ranked as high as No. 3 on the tou[r]
in 1967. Play, play, play.

The world listened when
Ashe spoke, whether about
his Davis Cup wins or global
social injustice.

A HERO'S JOURNEY

Arthur Ashe (1943–1993)

Anyone who'd met Arthur Ashe Jr. as a kid would never believe they were looking at a future champion, let alone one of the most important athletes in history. Scrawny, shy, and uncoordinated, Ashe was a bookworm and an easy target for bullies until he found tennis. "He was always kidded by the older boys," said his childhood pal from Richmond, Virginia, Beverly Colemen. "They would always slap him on his head and call him names ... He was under continuous stress at an early age."

Ashe, whose mother died when he was 6, began playing tennis early on at the Brookfield Park playground where his father was superintendent. "I was too small for any sport but tennis," Ashe wrote. "I learned to swim when I was very young, but I was always a bit afraid of water. My father wouldn't let me play football because of my size."

Ashe met his earliest mentor, Ron Charity, a Virginia University player, at the playground. Charity began instructing Ashe and eventually got him a membership at the all-black Richmond Racquet Club, where the well-to-do residents came to play and network. It was at the club that Ashe's awareness of race and class was aroused.

"It was difficult to tell whether Arthur was dragging the racket or the racket was dragging Arthur," said Charity. Nonetheless, he was impressed by Ashe's gumption. Charity introduced young Arthur to the man who would launch his career: Dr. Robert Johnson, perhaps the most influential man in the history of black tennis. Johnson was the founder of the American Tennis Association youth program and years earlier had coached Althea Gibson. Ashe's mind and game blossomed when he began playing

Though Ashe would lose
this third set at the 1975
Wimbledon to No.1-ranked
Jimmy Connors, he would
later take the crown.

"I was burning with resentment inside, but Dr.
Johnson had cautioned me not to show my anger."

—*Arthur Ashe*

at Johnson's home in Lynchburg, Virginia, where young black men and women were tutored and encouraged to earn tennis scholarships to college.

In 1955, Ashe earned his first title, the 12-and-under singles. He never looked back. Three years later, he was the first black kid to play in the Maryland Boys championship and went on to win the National Juniors and Boys championships in Kalamazoo, Michigan. The experience was sobering for the young Ashe. "When my father and some neighbors came to see me play, people sitting near them got up and moved. I was burning with resentment inside, but Dr. Johnson had cautioned me not to show my anger." Those lessons served him well throughout his career.

Both Johnson and Ashe were painfully aware that opportunities were limited for African-Americans who wanted a serious tennis career in the Jim Crow South. So, in 1960, with prodding from Johnson, a reluctant Ashe left home to train for a year in St. Louis, where there was no overt color line. The trip quickly paid off. In 1961, Ashe won the National Interscholastic Tennis championships singles title and soon after accepted a full scholarship to UCLA.

But racism followed him even to the intellectually elite campus. Shortly after arriving at college, Ashe was asked to sit out of a tournament because black players were not allowed to compete. Ashe quietly complied, but the racial inequality only reinforced his determination to fight for justice—and for wins. He was the first African-American to win an NCAA singles title and helped the Bruins clinch the NCAA tennis championship in 1965.

The sting of discrimination never swayed Ashe's love for America. He was especially proud when he was invited to become the first African-American to play on the U.S. Davis Cup team in 1963. "At the moment of my victory," Ashe wrote of a critical win against No. 8 Kenneth Fletcher of Australia, "it thrilled me beyond measure to hear the umpire announce not my name but that of my country." Ashe played on 10 Davis Cup squads over the next 15 years and, in 1981, became the team's first black captain.

After graduating from UCLA with a degree in business administration, Ashe joined the Army Reserves (he was honorably discharged in 1969 as a first lieutenant.) In 1968, Ashe won the U.S. Amateur and the U.S. Open. Two years later, he captured his second major title at the Australian Open.

The skinny kid from Richmond would never again be bullied. When the South African government denied him a visa to play in the South African Open in 1969, Ashe began his lifelong fight against government-sanctioned racism. With grace and dignity, the tennis legend became a leading voice against apartheid in South Africa and petitioned the International Lawn Tennis Federation to expel the racist nation. In 1973, after having his visa rejected three times, Ashe got his invite. Not only did he beome the first black person to win a doubles trophy in South Africa (with partner Tom Okker), but Ashe also spoke out passionately about the racism he saw there. This son of Jim Crow become an ardent advocate for the African National Congress and protested the imprisonment of Nelson Mandela. He was arrested outside the

"Today in pain, I should not be asking God, 'Why me?'"

—Arthur Ashe

South African embassy in Washington, D.C., for his efforts in 1985, but five years later the world celebrated as Nelson Mandela was released from prison. Ashe rejoiced at the end of apartheid in 1994, when Mandela was elected president under the first democratic elections.

Ashe's career was cut short by a 1979 heart attack, and the tennis icon retired in 1980 with 33 singles titles and 818 career wins. But Ashe's career in social justice was just beginning. In 1992 he was arrested again, this time outside the White House, for protesting the treatment of Haitian refugees. Ashe also founded several organizations, including the National Junior Tennis League, the ABC Cities Tennis Program, the Athlete-Career Connection, and the Safe Passage Foundation to promote tennis and education of underprivileged kids.

Ashe chose to beat *USA Today* to the punch on April 8, 1992, by announcing that he had contracted AIDS through a blood transfusion, at a time when ignorance and mass hysteria surrounded the disease. Ever the educator, Ashe reportedly responded to a fan who asked why God selected him for this awful disease by saying, "When I was holding a cup, I never asked God, 'Why me?' And today, in pain, I should not be asking God, 'Why me?'"

Until his death on February 6, 1993, at the age of 49, Arthur Ashe did what he always had: He eloquently fought the system by raising awareness and money to fight the disease that has ravaged millions. His legacy is a lesson for all skinny misfits: With courage and determination, Clark Kent can become Superman, and in the process make the world a more remarkable place.

GOLF

➡ BEFORE THE ROAR ⬅

John Shippen hid his race. Tiger deflects questions about it.

But in between, hundreds of African-Americans slowly chipped

away at pro golf's racist roots.

Tiger Woods
Woods, here at the Presidents
Cup in 2005, says he often reflects
back on the hard-won battles for
equality of groundbreakers like
Teddy Rhodes and Bill Spiller.

A TOUGH LIE

John Shippen Jr. (**1879–1968**)

John Shippen, who finished fifth in the second U.S. Open in 1896, is the first known African-American golf pro. But this fact wasn't made explicit until 18 years after his death, when his daughter Clara Johnson set the record straight with a *Pittsburgh Post-Gazette* reporter. Though he grew up on the Shinnecock Indian Reservation, where his father was a minister, Shippen was not half Native American, as was long believed. "My father was a Negro," Johnson told John H. Kennedy in *A Course of Their Own: A History of African-American Golfers*. "Every time I meet somebody, I have to correct that story [about his mixed race]." The ruse was manufactured by Theodore Havemeyer, the well-intentioned USGA president, who meant to quash complaints by white players who threatened to protest the 1896 Open if Shippen and Oscar Bunn, who really was Shinnecock, were allowed to play. Havemeyer told the appalled white golfers that the Open would take place with Shippen and Bunn or not at all. By participating, Shippen and Bunn also became the first American-born golfers to play in the U.S. Open.

Shippen golfed at the U.S. Open six times, the last in
1913. There would not be another black golfer at the
U.S. Open until Teddy Rhodes 35 years later.

A few months after teeing
off at the 1948 Los Angeles
Open, Rhodes would take
a legal swing at the PGA,
suing the organization for
barring black golfers from
entry into the Richmond
(California) Open.

ACCESS DENIED

Teddy Rhodes (1913–1969)

Teddy Rhodes thought things were improving by 1948. He had made the cut at the Los Angeles Open to continue on to the Richmond (California) Open. But when Rhodes, Bill Spiller, and Madison Gunter showed up, they were denied access to the greens because they were black. Incensed, the trio sued the PGA for $315,000 on the grounds that the PGA had deprived them of their livelihood based on race. Perhaps naively, they dropped the suit when the PGA promised to invite black players to their top tournaments. The PGA may have kept its word, had Rhodes not played so well at the U.S. Open that year.

When he opened with a 1-under-par 70 in the first round, just three strokes behind Ben Hogan, Rhodes created a panic because he "scared the hell out of some Southerners after that round," said Charles Miller, who presided over qualifying for the USGA for 40 years.

The Nashville native ultimately did muscle his way into 69 PGA events, finishing in the top 20 nine times. Unfortunately, by 1961, when the PGA rescinded the last vestiges of its whites-only clause, an ailing kidney had forced Rhodes into retirement. Still, he continued his fight by coaching the likes of Lee Elder and Althea Gibson. Poor health got the better of Rhodes on July 4, 1969, but his legacy has never died.

IN THE SWING

Ann Gregory (1912–1990)

Ann Gregory won the United Golf Association National Open Women's Championship a record five times, but when she arrived at her hotel before the 1963 Women's Amateur championship in Williamstown, Massachusetts, she was mistaken for a maid by fellow golfer Polly Riley. Gregory, who on September 17, 1956, became the first African-American woman to play in a USGA championship, took the slight with her usual aplomb. "Racism works best when you let it affect your mind," she said during her last national game in 1988. "For all the ugliness, I've gotten nice things three times over. I can't think ugly of anybody."

Bill Spiller (1913–1988)

Spiller, who began playing golf when he was nearly 30 years old, tallies up a 68 that ties Ben Hogan for second place at the first round of the Los Angeles Open. With Teddy Rhodes and Madison Gunther, Spiller sued the PGA for barring black golfers from PGA tournaments. The men dropped the suit after the PGA promised to change its policy. But it took the organization 13 more years to follow through.

GREEN DAY

Eldrick "Tiger"
Woods
(b.1975)

Back on April 8, 2001, when Woods was trying on his second Masters jacket (with an assist from the previous winner, Vijay Singh), he had the world at his feet. The win at Augusta—by two strokes over David Duval—gave him an unprecedented four majors in a row and six in all at the tender age of 25. But he was only on the front nine of his career. Since then, he has married, fathered two children, won eight more majors, downplayed his role as a trailblazer—and suffered a major hit to his All-American image. It remains to be seen if he can surpass Jack Nicklaus in majors (18), or win back the public. But he has been known to recover on the back nine.

Sifford's sudden-death
triumph over South
Africa's Harold Henning
at the 1969 Los Angeles
Open was still not enough
to get him an invitation
to the all-white Masters.

UPHILL BATTLE

Charlie Sifford (b.1922)

"There is no place for a black man in professional golf," wrote the PGA's first African-American tour winner in his 1992 autobiography *Just Let Me Play*. But it didn't stop Charlie Sifford from muscling his way into golf's history books.

Born in Charlotte, North Carolina, in 1922, Sifford, like most black players of the time, caught the golfing bug as a caddy. Even in the Jim Crow South, his talent attracted such unexpected supporters as future PGA pro Clayton Heafner and Sutton Alexander, owner of the Carolina Country Club where Sifford caddied. Recognizing potential in Sifford's self-taught game, Heafner and Alexander began formally teaching him. But Alexander's white patrons and even his white staffers didn't take to a black man teeing off on their links.

One greenskeeper followed Sifford and shot a starter gun whenever Sifford teed off. Fearing violence was imminent, Alexander urged Sifford's parents to send him North. So, in 1939, following a minor scuffle with the law, Sifford moved to Philadelphia.

Relocating to Philly didn't just save Sifford's life, it radically improved his game. Playing against seasoned pros like six-time National Negro Open champ Howard Wheeler and four-time National Negro Open champ Teddy Rhodes stoked Sifford's ambition. He wanted to be more than a local hero. After a tour of duty in World War II, Sifford befriended famed jazz singer Billy Eckstine after they were introduced by Rhodes. As Eckstine's personal golf pro and valet, Sifford entered a new world. According to Sifford, "I was able to play at private clubs

and had access to various golf courses because of my relationship with Billy."

Dominating the black circuit didn't satisfy Sifford, who held the UGA national title six times from 1948 to 1960. He wanted to prove he could win an unsegregated event, and did just that at the Long Beach Open in 1957, when he topped Eric Monti to become the first African-American to win a PGA-sponsored event. Still, most other tournaments refused him. Under public pressure from the likes of Jackie Robinson and California Attorney General Stanley Mosk, the PGA finally granted Sifford his tour card in 1960, the first issued to an African-American.

In 1967, more than 30 years after hauling his first golf bag for a white player, Sifford charged from five strokes back on the final day to win the Greater Hartford Open and the $20,000 winner's purse. Neither that win, nor any other, would secure Sifford an invitation to the Masters. The Caucasian-only clause was gone, but its spirit remained.

It still rankles Sifford that he retired before the PGA changed its rules to grant automatic entry to the Masters to winners of specific tourneys. But being the first African-American inducted into the World Golf Hall of Fame in 2004 seems to have assuaged some of the pain. "I'm in the Hall of Fame," said Sifford during his induction speech. "And that's better than the Masters."

"I'm in the Hall of Fame. And that's better than the Masters."

—Charlie Sifford

OPPOSITE PAGE
That's not a smile on Sifford's face. While he led the first 45 holes at the 1969 Los Angeles Open, Sifford grimaced after missing a short putt by an inch on the eighth hole.

After Elder won the 1974
Monsanto Open with an 18-foot
birdie putt on the final hole of
a sudden-death playoff with
Peter Oosterhuis, his next
historic stop was the
1975 Masters.

MASTER
PLAN

Lee Elder (b.1934)

Lee Elder, the first African-American to crash the gates of Augusta, winner of four PGA and eight Senior PGA events, the ever-modest elder statesman of the links, cut his teeth hustling on the all-white greens of Dallas, Texas. His marks could only blame themselves; that's what they got for underestimating a guy who'd been caddying since he was 9 years old to put food on his family's table. Assuming he was a kid, a black kid, they thought he couldn't possibly beat them at their own game. What these privileged white men didn't know was that Elder's mentor was Alvin "Titanic" Thompson, an infamous flim-flam man. Thompson would con these men into wagering a few holes against his "chauffeur." They never suspected they were being schooled by a young man who would one day play with the likes of Jack Nicklaus and bust the color barrier at the Masters.

"If I gave up, who was going to continue the struggle?"

—*Lee Elder*

Elder didn't start out with a master plan. Born in Dallas in 1934, Elder, one of eight siblings, lost both his parents in 1944—his father died in World War II and his mother, heartbroken, died three months later. Elder began working as a caddy at the all-white Tennison Park Golf Club to add to the family's meager pot. By the time he began caddying (and shilling) for Titanic Thompson as a teenager, he'd cobbled together a set of mismatched clubs and honed his backswing by sneaking onto blind spots on the Tennison course. Eventually, Thompson saw an even bigger score: he'd encourage Elder's legit early career.

With some cash in hand, Elder took his game to the National Negro Open in Cleveland. He lost to Joe Louis but won a life-long connection to the retired heavyweight-turned-golf-pro when he befriended Louis' golf coach, Teddy Rhodes. After a stint in the Army from 1959 to 1961, Elder saw the ultimate legit angle: Tournament victories and a side gig as an instructor earned him the $6,500 the PGA required to enroll in its qualifying school. By 1967 he'd won five United Golf Association championships and finally joined the Tour the following year at the Monsanto Open, in Pensacola, Florida.

But there were no cheers for Elder and other black golfers, like Pete Brown, who had to change their clothes and eat their meals in parking lots and use the caddy restroom. "It's so hard to continue to fight when every time you go into a place you get a shotgun stuck in your face," Elder told *USA Today* in 2000, "or have someone saying, 'Nigger, get out of here' ... I was the youngest black pro out there ... I had a lot of other people telling me that if I gave up, who was going to continue the struggle?" Elder wouldn't play in the shadows for long. In 1968, he took Jack Nicklaus to sudden-death at the American Golf Classic. Nicklaus won on the fifth playoff hole, but no one would ever mistake Elder for a chauffeur again.

But Elder still had one hurdle left: to qualify for a shot at the Green Jacket. He leaped over that hurdle at the 1974 Monsanto Open, where six years earlier he was forced to dress in the parking lot. He birdied three of the last four holes to force a playoff with Peter Oosterhuis. Elder won the tournament with a dramatic 18-foot birdie putt on the fourth playoff hole, clincing a spot in the 1975 Masters.

Although Elder would play in five more Masters, win three more PGA tournaments, and become the first black member of the Ryder Cup team in 1979, his 1975 breakthrough was what stood out for at least one up-and-comer. "I'm the first, but I wasn't the pioneer," Tiger Woods said after he won the Masters in 1997. "Charlie Sifford, Lee Elder, Teddy Rhodes, those guys paved the way for me to be here."

HORSE RACING

⟹ HIGH STAKES ⟸

Black riders like Oliver Lewis, Isaac Murphy, Willie Simms,

and Jimmy Winkfield were the front-runners of American

horse racing. Then, just like that, African-American jockeys

were left in the dust.

Jimmy Winkfield
Winner of the 1901 and 1902 Kentucky Derbies, Winkfield cut a striking figure in the world of horse racing, first in the U.S. and then in Europe.

Lewis poses circa 1875
to commemorate his win
aboard Aristides in the
inaugural Kentucky Derby.

THE PACESETTER

Oliver Lewis (1856–1924)

No one was more astonished than Oliver Lewis when his mount, Aristides, won the first Kentucky Derby in 1875 at what was then called the Louisville Jockey Club. Owner H.P. McGrath had entered Aristides merely as a pace-setter for another one of his horses, the highly favored Chesapeake, ridden by William Henry. But Chesapeake never caught up to Aristides and Lewis, one of 13 black jockeys in the 15-horse field, and by the final stretch, the favorite had fallen far behind. Easing up, Lewis looked to McGrath at trackside for instruction; McGrath waved Lewis on. In front of 10,000 spectators, Lewis and Aristides won the Derby by two lengths ahead of Volcano in a record-setting 2 minutes 37.75 seconds. (At the time, the Derby was 1.5 miles long. It would be shortened to 1.25 miles in 1896.)

Later that year, Lewis rode Aristides to second place at the Belmont Stakes, and he'd gather two more wins at the Louisville Jockey Club by the end of the season. Though he'd never ride in the Derby again, Lewis ultimately used his exceptional racing knowledge and stable connections to provide information to bookmakers, who were then legal in the U.S. He'd later become a bookie himself and created a system of handicapping similar to what the *Daily Racing Form* still uses today.

CROUCHING TIGER

Willie Simms (1870–1927)

If you were a betting man in the late 19th century, the smart money was on whatever mount Willie Simms was riding. One of the earliest jockeys to ride short stirrups, wherein the rider squats tightly over the horse's shoulders, Simms captured nearly 25% of his 4,532 races in a 15-year career. He took the Belmont Stakes crown aboard Commanche in 1893, then repeated the next year on two-time Horse of the Year Henry of Navarre. Simms was also the first American to win an English race aboard an American horse. In the process, he became the first to popularize the crouching posture with British riders.

Back in the States, Simms won the Kentucky Derby twice, aboard Ben Brush in 1896 (the first year the shorter 1.25-mile course was introduced), and in 1898 aboard Plaudit. A few weeks later, while riding Sly Fox at the 1898 Preakness, Simms galloped past the finish line—and into the history books—as the only African-American ever to take all three Triple Crown races.

With one of the most outstanding records of the era, Simms should have been inducted into the Racing Hall of Fame in its inaugural year of 1950. But it took until 1977 for Simms' contributions to be recognized by the Hall. To date, he, Isaac Murphy, and Jimmy Winkfield are the only African-Americans to have been admitted.

Simms, pictured here in 1894, was hardly the only African-American trailblazer on the road to the Roses. Between 1875 and 1902, black jockeys won 15 of 28 Kentucky Derbies.

RIDING AWAY

Jimmy Winkfield (1880–1974)

When Jimmy Winkfield won the Kentucky Derby on May 3, 1902, aboard Alan-a-Dale, it was the last time a black jockey would take home the coveted ring of roses. The former Kentucky stable boy made four consecutive Derby runs, taking third in 1900, first in 1901 and 1902, and second in 1903. Winkfield was blacklisted after breaking a contract with owner John Madden and taking a $3,000 deal to ride Highball for W.M. Scheftel in the 1903 Futurity in Saratoga. Wink had already raised the ire of his white counterparts for his success, so after his blatant move for more money, angry white jockeys began plotting to keep him out of races. Worse, white riders attacked Winkfield and the other black jockeys when they did ride. Stable owners, fearing injury to their horses, pulled their black jockeys out of races—a move that watered down the competition and opened the door for more whites to compete and win. Rather than being relegated to stablehand, Winkfield packed his bags and headed overseas, where he eventually became an international star in Europe, dying in France at the age of 94.

Shortly after his 1902 Derby win, Winkfield, pictured here atop Pentecost circa 1901, packed his bags for Russia, where he won the national title three times. Later, he moved to France and married a Russian heiress.

BACK IN
THE SADDLE

Marlon St. Julien (b.1972)

Marlon St. Julien understands his place in history. In 2000, he was the first black jockey to race in the Kentucky Derby since African-Americans were effectively banned from the sport 79 years earlier. St. Julien's fifth-place ride at the Kentucky Oaks was the first appearance in that race by a black jockey in 103 years. "That era [when blacks starred] is a spot in the past that really isn't recognized," St. Julien told the *Cincinnati Enquirer* in 2002. "I'm very respectful of that past. Just thinking about them makes me want to bring more success in their name." At the peak of his career, the Louisiana native rode Curule to a seventh-place finish in the 2000 Kentucky Derby and ranked 33rd on the money list, riding horses that won more than $5.8 million. Though nearing retirement, St. Julien still rides in local races. In 2007, he rode a 49-1 odds mount, I Are Sharp, to victory in the $50,000 Premiere Stakes at Lone Star Park in Grand Prairie, Texas. Two years later, he earned his 2,000th career victory at Delta Downs in Louisiana.

St. Julien had dreams of playing football when he was a kid. When he topped out at 5'4" as a teen, he switched gears and began riding at Evangeline Downs (Louisiana) in 1989.

COME-FROM-BEHIND

Isaac Murphy (1860–1896)

Isaac Murphy, the first jockey inducted into the National Museum of Racing's Hall of Fame, was also one of the first black athletes to be paid his due in the 19th century—at least for a time. Earning up to $15,000 per year at the peak of his career in the 1880s, Murphy became a superstar for innovating a nail-biting strategy on the track: Rather than pushing hard throughout an entire race, Murphy tended to conserve his horse's energy to get a burst of speed during the final stretch.

Murphy rode his way into history as the first jockey to win the Kentucky Derby three times—in 1884 aboard Buchanan and back-to-back in 1890 and 1891 with Riley and Kingman. His estimated career winning percentage of .447—a reported 628 victories in 1,412 starts—is still the gold standard in racing. He was also known to be unshakably ethical. During the 1879 Kenner Stakes, he refused to take a loss atop champion Falsetto despite substantial incentives from gamblers.

What isn't unusual about Murphy's stunning career was the matter of his race. In fact, African-Americans dominated horse racing for most of the 19th century. "By 1800 in the South, the vast majority of jockeys were diminutive slaves who had grown up around horses all their lives," wrote Arthur R. Ashe Jr. in *A Hard Road to Glory: A History of the African-American Athlete.* It was reported that 13 of 15 jockeys in the first Kentucky Derby, on May 17, 1875, were black, including the winner, Oliver Lewis.

Thanks in large part to Murphy and other great black riders, horse racing became ever more popular and

profitable in the 1880s. Murphy pocketed not just the
flat fees for races, but, later in his career, a share of
the horse's winnings. In one ballyhooed match race, on
June 25, 1890, Murphy won a $10,000 purse aboard
Salvator against Snapper Garrison, who rode Tenny.

But as the purses increased, white jockeys began to edge
out the African-American champs, including Murphy. The
increased pressure and a burgeoning drinking problem
began to take its toll on Murphy. On August 26, 1890, he
was suspended for a month after a drunken ride at
Monmouth, when he finished last aboard the champion
Firenze. To make matters worse, Murphy's weight

"The largest funeral ever
seen here over a colored
person was that held
on Sunday when Isaac
Murphy, the famous
jockey, was buried."

—*The New York Times,* February 1896

"By 1800 in the South, the vast majority of jockeys were diminutive slaves who had grown up around horses all their lives."

—*Arthur R. Ashe Jr.*

fluctuated wildly. His last crash diet before the 1896 season made him so ill that he caught pneumonia—he died just shy of his 36th birthday.

In his final years Murphy was forced to jostle for a place in the sport he'd helped transform. But nearly 500 mourners turned out for his funeral. *The New York Times* reported in 1896, "The largest funeral ever seen here over a colored person was that held on Sunday when Isaac Murphy, the famous jockey, was buried ... The funeral procession was one of the longest ever seen in Lexington."

Murphy, who won four American Derbies and three Kentucky Derbies, hobnobs with white attendees at the Salvator Clambake in 1890.

TRACK & FIELD

➡ FAST AND FURIOUS ⬅

The Tigerbelles made huge strides. Tommie Smith and John

Carlos took a stand. And Carl Lewis and Gail Devers highlighted

a golden age for the purest of all sports.

Carl Lewis
Lewis leaped to his second
of four gold medals at
the 1984 Olympics, with
a 28-foot, ¼-inch long jump
on his first attempt.

In 1924, Gourdin added
another medal to his
formidable collection—
an Olympic silver in
the broad jump.

HEAVY MEDAL

Edward Gourdin (1897–1966)

Twenty-five feet, three inches. Edward Gourdin's broad-jump record stunned the track world 15 years before Jesse Owens brought home the gold at the 1936 Olympics. Ned still holds the Harvard record from that 1921 Oxford-Cambridge meet—where he also won the 100-yard dash (10.2 seconds). Gourdin, the first athlete to broad-jump more than 25 feet, had come to Harvard from Stanton High School in Jacksonville, Florida, where he was the valedictorian. According to some accounts, Gourdin won so many medals at Harvard that when he graduated, the school—unable to cast the medals fast enough—still owed him five golds.

But the lanky leaper had much more to accomplish. In 1924 Gourdin graduated from Harvard Law and won the silver medal in the broad jump at the Paris Olympics. After serving in World War II as a colonel, Gourdin was appointed an assistant district attorney in Boston, and eventually he became the first black person to be seated on the Massachusetts Superior Court, where he served until his death in 1966.

GLOBE TROTTER

Malvin Whitfield (b.1924)

Malvin Whitfield is nothing if not a man of the world. At the 1948 Olympics in London, Whitfield (pictured in the lead at left), won the 800 meters. "The Olympic medal alone will keep a winner warm for a lifetime," he said, still damp from the rain-soaked race. A few days later, the first active serviceman to win Olympic gold got another for his stretch in the 4x400-meter relay. While serving in the Air Force during the Korean War, Whitfield held track clinics in Tokyo for Japanese runners and trained on the runways in preparation for the Pan American Games. His tarmac regime worked; in Buenos Aires he won three golds, in the 400, 800, and 1,600 meters. In Helsinki at the 1952 Summer Games, Whitfield repeated as champion of the 800 meters, winning his third Olympic gold.

But these international jaunts were just layovers in Marvelous Mal's life abroad. After winning 66 of 69 midrange races from 1946 to 1955 and setting six world records, Whitfield retired from competition to join the U.S. Information Agency as a diplomat and sports trainer. After getting his bachelor of science degree at California State University, Los Angeles, he was named sports advisor to Liberian President William V. Shadrack Tubman.

Traveling to more than 132 countries during his illustrious career with the State Department, Whitfield also headed up programs such as an African pre-Olympic training camp in Somalia in 1972. "It will be 50 years before Africa takes its full place in sports," he told *The New York Times*. "If patience means cool, you've got to be chilly in Africa." (He underestimated racial progress slightly; South Africa hosted the 2010 World Cup.)

At the 1996 Centennial Olympics in Atlanta. Whitfield was honored as one of the greatest 100 living American Olympians. Another member of the "Golden 100," sprinter Bob Hayes, said of Whitfield, "He is a friend, a brother, and a mentor. When we were coming up out of the ghettos, he took care of us. We not only like him, we love him."

HIGH BAR

Alice Coachman (b.1923)

Despite her 10 consecutive national high jump titles from 1939 to 1948, Alice Coachman was always down-to-earth about her great feats. "From the very first gold medal I won in 1939, my mama used to stress being humble," she told *The New York Times* in 1995. "You're no better than anyone else. The people you pass on the ladder will be the same people you'll be with when the ladder comes down." As it turned out, though, Coachman moved in only one direction: up. Even before her first class at Tuskegee Institute, she won her first of 25 national AAU track titles, in the high jump, and she would go on to win the 50- and 100-meter dashes and 4x100-meter relay. During the off-season, she won three conference championships for the basketball team. Because war cancelled the 1940 and 1944 Olympics, Coachman had to wait until 1948 to become the first black woman ever named to a U.S. Olympic team. Setting the Olympic record with a 5-foot, 6⅛-inch high jump at the London Games, Coachman also became the first black woman ever to win Olympic gold. And then she retired. She still had the hops, but she felt she had simply climbed to the top rung of that particular ladder. Besides, Coachman had other, less conspicuous goals in mind. For the next 40 years, Coachman taught elementary and high school students in Albany, Georgia, and in 1994, she established the Alice Coachman Track and Field Foundation, an organization dedicated to giving a boost to future and former Olympians.

At the 1948 Games, Coachman broke a women's Olympic record in the high jump—and became the first black woman in history to take home an Olympic gold medal.

FIRST STEPS

William Harrison
"Bones" Dillard
(b.1923)

When Dillard first saw Jesse
Owens in a Cleveland parade
to celebrate Owens' four 1936
Olympic golds, the gangly
13-year-old knew he'd found
his life's calling. What he
didn't know was that soon
after, he'd not only meet his
newfound hero, but Owens
would be the one to give him
his first pair of sneakers.
Pictured far left winning the
100-meter dash at the 1948
Olympics in a record-tying
10.3 seconds with Barney
Ewell (number 70) close
behind, Dillard would go on
to earn another two golds
in the 1948 and 1952 4x100-
meter relays. His fourth
Olympic gold, a 1952 win in
the 110-meter hurdles, is
still unprecedented: Dillard
is the only athlete to win
Olympic crowns in both
sprinting and hurdling.

BORN TO RUN

Wilma Rudolph (1940–1994)

She wasn't supposed to walk, much less become one of the fastest women in the world. But Wilma Rudolph's mother refused to let her sixth of eight children languish because of polio. "My doctors told me I would never walk again," said Rudolph, who had 21 half and full siblings. "My mother told me I would. I believed my mother."

After doggedly struggling through physical therapy to strengthen her left leg, Rudolph eventually led her Burt High School (Clarksville, Tennessee) basketball squad to a state championship. By her sophomore year she caught the eye of Ed Temple, Tennessee State's famed track coach, who invited her to the Tigerbelles' summer training camp. By 16, the girl who couldn't walk without leg braces as a child had won bronze in the 4x100-meters in the 1956 Olympics. At the 1960 Olympics in Rome, Rudolph took home three golds for the 100 meters, 200 meters, and 4x100-meter relay, and set two records: an Olympic mark of 23.2 seconds in a 200-meter heat and, together with her running mates, the world record of 44.4 seconds in the 4x100-meter relay semifinal.

In 6.9 seconds, the Tennessee State Tigerbelle set a new U.S. women's indoor record for the 60-yard dash at the 1961 Los Angeles Invitational.

Mildred McDaniel
(1933–2004)

Out-jumping her closest competitor by more than 3 inches, McDaniel of Tuskegee Institute set the new world record in women's high jump with a stunning 5-foot, 9¼-inch roll for an Olympic gold at the 1956 Melbourne Games.

PRESIDENTIAL RACE

LeRoy Walker (b.1918)

When Dr. LeRoy Walker was elected president of the United States Olympic Committee in 1992, he had gold-medal credentials: He held a doctorate from New York University and had served in various USOC executive posts. At North Carolina Central University, where he had coached track, football, and basketball starting in 1945, he helped produce 111 All-Americas and 12 track and field Olympians, including 1976 gold-winning 400-meter hurdler Edwin Moses (pictured with Walker at right).

Walker, though, did not think of his color as a qualification. "Of course, there's a certain amount of pride of being the first African-American to serve as president," he told *The New York Times*, "But ... it's good to hear that I was nominated for what I've done, rather than what I am."

From the start of his four-year term, Walker made clear that he had little tolerance for commercialism from corporations and professional leagues. Walker also had little patience for athletes who complained about losing. The previous summer's Dream Team appalled him on both counts. "After five minutes, [fans] turned off the basketball games," Walker said. "It was like watching the Globetrotters." He wrangled with leagues to trim the number of pros and include more elite amateurs.

But Walker also took his lumps. An assistant to the president, Dr. Evie Dennis, publicly criticized the USOC for the number of blacks and women on the board. "It seems to me the committee thinks naming a black president is all it's got to do," she said, pointing to the 24 women and 11 African-Americans (including two women) on the 99-member board. Point taken. Walker set up task forces to address the problem. "The buck stops here," said Walker. Twelve years after Walker retired, the board had been cut down to 11 members, nearly half of whom were women and/or black.

Rather than boycotting the 1968
Olympics, Smith (middle on podium) and
Carlos (right) took the gold and bronze,
respectively, in the 200 meters—and a
stand for African-American rights.

SHOCK WAVE

Tommie Smith (**b.1944**) and John Carlos (**b.1945**)

Tommie Smith and John Carlos weren't exactly sure what they would do when they took the podium at the 1968 Olympic ceremony to receive their respective gold and bronze medals in the 200-meter race. Each had a black glove ready to symbolize black power and unity. Smith had his box containing an olive branch to signify peace. Carlos wore black beads around his neck to represent the thousands of anonymous African-Americans who were lynched at the hands of white racists. But it wasn't until just before the race that they put the finishing touch on what would go down as one of the most politically potent protests in Olympic history. "We decided in that tunnel that if we were going to go out on that stand, we were going to go out barefooted," said Carlos in 2003. "We wanted the world to know that in Mississippi, Alabama, Tennessee, South Central Los Angeles, Chicago, that people were still walking back and forth in poverty without even the necessary clothes to live." Atop the podium, they raised gloved fists.

Both men had considered boycotting the Games altogether. "I am quite willing not only to give up participation in the Games but my life as well, if necessary, to open a door by which the oppression and injustices suffered by black people in the U.S. might be alleviated," Smith said a few months before the Olympics. In 2003 Carlos explained, "Not everyone was down with that plan [to boycott]. A lot of the athletes thought that winning medals would supercede or protect them from racism."

Though both Smith and Carlos were active in the black movement on the campus of San Jose State University, neither was a Black Panther, as was reported at the time, nor did they identify with militants. But their silent protest was met with outrage. They were banned from the Olympic Village and temporarily suspended from the U.S. team, and worse, they and their families were subjected to death threats. Smith, who'd hold the world record until 1971 for his gold medal 200-meter run in 19.83 seconds, was shocked by the rage. "We were not anti-Christs," Smith said in the HBO documentary *Fists of Freedom*. "We were just human beings who saw a need to be recognized ... There was nothing but a raised fist in the air and a bowed head, acknowledging the American flag—not symbolizing a hatred for it."

In 2008, Smith and Carlos were awarded the Arthur Ashe Award, ESPN's highest sports humanitarian honor.

FAST LIFE

Florence Griffith-Joyner (**1959–1998**)

With the wind at her back at the 1988 Seoul Olympics, Griffith-Joyner won gold in the 100-meter sprint in 10.54 seconds. Not that she needed any help. In the Olympic trials and the quarterfinal, she'd already run the three fastest 100-meter times ever for a woman. (The fastest, 10.49 seconds, is still a record.) In the 200-meter final, the long-taloned beauty clocked a still-standing record of 21.34 seconds. Only Marion Jones' 21.63-second World Cup dash has come close. Flo-Jo's final Olympic run in the 4x100-meter relay would be her last gold before she retired from track. Sadly, the fastest woman in the world died at 38 years old, after suffering a seizure in her sleep.

PRIDE IN STRIDE

Carl Lewis (b.1961)

With nine Olympic golds in his pocket, you'd think any one of the four Games Carl Lewis conquered would be his proudest achievement. Perhaps it was the 1984 Games, when the brash hoofer won the 100-meter race by 0.2 seconds and earned a second gold in the long jump by leaping 28 feet, ¼ inch on his first attempt, then reaping boos for skipping his last four tries after he knew he had it sewn up. "He rubs it in too much," said Edwin Moses, the two-time gold medalist in the 400-meter hurdles. "A little humility is in order." Unhumbly, Lewis took home two more golds—in the 200 meters and the 4x100-meter relay—matching Jesse Owens' Olympic tally in 1936.

Perhaps his finest hour came in 1988, when Lewis earned two more Olympic golds in the long jump and the 100-meter dash. Or in Barcelona in 1992, when he reclaimed the long-jump title that Mike Powell had taken at the 1991 World Athletic Championships, and added Gold No. 8 for the 4x100-meter relay. Or was it in 1996 at the Atlanta Games, where the 35-year-old earned his ninth gold medal in the long jump?

No, the victory he savors the most is his 100-meter win at the '91 World Athletic Championships. Lewis plowed past six runners, all of whom came in under 10 seconds. "He passed us like we were standing still," said runner-up Leroy Burrell. And he set a new world record (since broken) with 9.86 seconds. "The best race of my life," Lewis said. "The best technique, the fastest. And I did it at 30."

Lewis reflects back on this 100-meter win at the 1991 World Athletic Championships as his greatest accomplishment—despite having his 10-year winning streak in the long jump snapped by Mike Powell at the same event.

ON POINT

Jackie Joyner-Kersee (b.1962)

She was the first woman to top 7,000 points in the heptathlon—the grueling seven-sport event consisting of the 100-meter hurdles, high jump, shot put, 200-meter dash, long jump, javelin, and 800-meter race. Joyner-Kersee still holds the top five highest scores and the world record with 7,291 points won at the 1988 Olympics. At the 1992 U.S. Olympic Trials (pictured right), Joyner-Kersee would tally just 6,695— her lowest score in seven years—but she still won the event by 400 points. With six Olympic medals— three of them gold— Joyner-Kersee joined sister-in-law Florence Griffith-Joyner in the vanguard of the first generation to benefit from Title IX. But as Bruce Jenner, the 1976 Olympic decathlon champ, said, "She's the greatest multievent athlete ever, man or woman."

LONG LEGS

Gail Devers
(b.1966)

Gail Devers has never understood quit. When she was diagnosed with Graves' disease in 1990, her doctors thought they'd have to amputate when the thyroid condition caused debilitating swelling in her feet. But 17 months later in Barcelona, Devers won her first Olympic gold, in the 100-meter dash. Had she not stumbled on the final gate of the 100-meter hurdles, she would have won a second. Devers avenged that loss in 1993, taking seven titles, including the 100-meter dash and the 100-meter hurdles at the Worlds. In 1996, she earned her second Olympic gold in the 100-meter race and another in the 4x100-meter relay. In 2007, at age 40, Devers took the 60-meter hurdle crown at the Millrose Games. "People talk about retiring," said Devers after her 7.86-second Millrose win, "I never said that r-word."

UNSTOPPABLE

Michael Johnson
(b.1967)

At the 1996 Olympics, when Michael Johnson shattered his own world record of 19.66 seconds—set at the Olympic trials just weeks before—even he was astonished at his nearly supernatural 19.32-second 200-meter dash. "I can't describe what it feels like to break the world record by that much," Johnson said at the time. "I thought 19.5 was possible, but 19.3 is unbelievable.'" Bronze medalist Ato Boldon was so awed that he literally bowed before the eventual nine-time world champion, who had days before won the 400 meters in an Olympic record 43.49 seconds. "I said earlier that the man who wins the 100 meters is the fastest man alive," Boldon remarked. Gesturing to Johnson, he added, "But now I think the fastest man alive is sitting to my left." (The gold-shod wonder's record stood for 12 years, until Usain Bolt bettered it in Beijing in 2008.) Johnson would also win a fourth gold in the 400 at the 2000 Games in Sydney.

FOR WHOM THE 'BELLES TOLL

Edward Temple (b.1927)

In 1950, more than 20 years before Title IX granted women the same opportunity to compete for athletic scholarships as men, Edward Temple hit the ground running in the fight for women's rights. As head coach of the Tennessee State Tigerbelles until 1994, he created one of the most accomplished programs in the history of track and field, collecting an astonishing 23 Olympic medals, 34 national championships, and 30 Pan American Games medals.

Truth is, no one expected much from the women's team when Temple took over as TSU's track and field coach— it was just part of the deal the university made with their masters of science candidate for an associate professorship. That, along with working in the school's post office. With just a handful of girls, an unfinished track, and a $300 budget, Temple built the Tigerbelles

From the get-go, Temple (center) inspired the newly anointed Tigerbelles to win at the highest levels. In 1953, just three years after he took over as coach, 'Belles (from left) Wilma Rudolph, Isabelle Daniels, Willie B. White, Lucinda Williams, Mae Faggs, and Margaret Matthews were Olympics-bound.

into a world-class team. "Nobody else wanted the job," Temple told *USA Today* in 1993. "For years, other coaches would ask me, 'Why are you dealing with the women?' "

For Temple, who grew up in an integrated working-class neighborhood in Harrisburg, Pennsylvania, the answer was simple. "Equal means equal," he said later. "It means the same thing at the same time at the same place. Everyone should have the same opportunity." He was so galvanized by the paucity of resources for the women's team that after three seasons, Temple quit coaching the men's team altogether to focus solely on the 'Belles.

Until 1967, Temple had no scholarships at all to offer his recruits. Instead, the whip-cracking coach pitched a guaranteed job; grueling year-round, three-a-day practices; and the chance to win. But his charges had to follow his rules: earn good grades, no dating during the season, and absolutely no unladylike behavior. The young women had to wear dresses and gloves outside of practice or track meets. No exceptions.

Facing harsh Jim Crow laws and a culture that undermined female athletes, the ladies encountered enormous challenges before they even hit the blocks. As the coach recalls, "My first year we only had one track meet a year, on a cinder track. When we would go on trips to such places as the Tuskegee Relays, we couldn't stop at any gasoline stations, so we had to get out of the van and hit the field to go to the restroom. But still, when it came time to represent the country, they were right there."

They did more than represent. The Tigerbelles won. Just two years after Temple took the helm, his first recruit, Mae Faggs, brought home Olympic gold in the 4x100-meter relay along with Janet Moreau, Catherine Hardy, and 15-year-old Barbara Jones—the youngest woman to win an Olympic gold medal in track and field. In 1960, in Rome, Tigerbelle Wilma Rudolph became the first female athlete to win three golds at the same Olympics, capturing

In the semifinals at the 1960 Olympics, Tigerbelles (left to right) Wilma Rudolph, Lucinda Williams, Barbara Jones, and Martha Hudson broke the world record for the 400-meter relay in 44.4 seconds. Including the 'Belles eventual relay gold, Rudolph collected three firsts at the Rome Games.

> "Equal means equal. It means the same thing at the same time at the same place."
>
> —Ed Temple

the 100 meters, 200 meters, and 4x100-meter relay races. "I was so happy," said Coach Temple of Rudolph's trifecta, "I was bursting all the buttons off my shirt."

Since then, eight of his charges have been inducted into the National Track and Field Hall of Fame, including two-time Olympic gold medalist Chandra Cheeseborough, to whom Temple passed the coaching torch in 1994.

So after fielding 40 Olympians, winning 34 national titles, and gleaning incalculable recognition for women's sports in general, what does Temple have to say about his 44-year career? "Twenty-eight [of my Olympians] got their master's degree and 14 got either an M.D. or PhD. What more could you ask for?"

While German officials, spectators, and silver medalist Lutz Long hailed Hitler, Jesse Owens saluted America on August 4, 1936, during the medal ceremony for the long jump at the Berlin Olympics.

CROWN OF THORNS

Jesse Owens (1913–1980)

With his laurel-leafed triumph over Hitler's Aryan athletes at the 1936 Berlin Olympics, Jesse Owens became a resounding symbol of American ideals—of the truths of life, liberty, and justice for all. His lone American salute on the podium in a sea of Nazi *heils* was a moment whose tragic meaning would not be fully known for another 10 years. And yet, back at home, Owens was treated little better than chattel, used as a propaganda tool, and then dismissed by the USOC.

Americans swelled with pride with Owens' first gold, a world record 10.3-second 100-meter win over fellow African-American Ralph Metcalfe. Even Germans cheered as he dashed past the finish line. The track phenom went on to take the long jump crown with a world record leap of 26 feet, $5\frac{5}{16}$ inches against German Lutz Long. Owens

At the 1935 Big Ten Western Conference Outdoor Track and Field Meet, Owens broke three world records in a 45-minute span. Here, he breaks the 220-yard dash mark in a blistering 20.3 seconds. Later, he'd take out the 220-yard hurdle record with a time of 22.6 seconds, and then he would set the broad jump world record with an astonishing leap of 26 feet, 8½ inches.

also took the top medal in the 200-meter race with a time of 20.7 seconds (yet another world record) and the 4x100-meter relay. But the praise he received frequently came with a terrible modifier. "Owens was black as tar, but what the hell," said novelist Thomas Wolfe, "It was our team and I thought he was wonderful."

The 22-year-old hero didn't have long to bask in his Olympic glory. "I came back to my native country and I couldn't ride in the front of the bus," said Owens. "I had to go to the back door. I couldn't live where I wanted. I wasn't invited to shake hands with Hitler, but I wasn't invited to the White House to shake hands with the president either." Unlike today, Olympians did not have the right to personally capitalize on their fame. There would be no Wheaties box covers, no appearances on late-night TV, no endorsement deals for Owens. Instead, the day after the Olympics wrapped up, the fleet-footed symbol of democracy was compelled by the American Athletic Union and the U.S. Olympic Committee to participate in track exhibitions throughout Europe. While Owens earned nothing for these appearances, the AAU took a reported 15% of the gate proceeds.

With no money for food or train fare, let alone cash to send home to his wife and child, Owens reluctantly joined the tour, but several days later, exhausted, dejected, and 11 pounds thinner, Owens had had enough. He packed up and took a boat back home. "All we athletes get out of this Olympic business is a view out of a train or airplane window," Owens told *The Chicago Defender* shortly after his return from Berlin. "This track business is becoming one of the biggest rackets in the world. The AAU gets the money." And had all the power. Furious that Owens had left the tour and had fielded sponsorship

offers, the AAU and USOC banished the Olympian for life from official competition.

This son of sharecroppers spent the next 16 years chasing any work he could get to support his growing family. Reduced to little more than a circus attraction, Owens raced baseball players, trains, horses, and even a dog for a paycheck. But these degradations took a heavy toll. "Those races made me sick," Owens said years later, "I felt like a freak." His family watched in horror at the indignities he suffered. "It was a terrible time for him," his youngest daughter, Marlene Owens Rankin, told *The Guardian* in 2000. "They took away his career. They took away his life ... Can you imagine how Tiger would feel, and how the rest of the world would react, if he was told at 24 he could never hit another golf ball again in serious competition?"

Later in life, Owens would achieve a greater stature, if not the payday he deserved for his accomplishments. In 1955 he was appointed sports ambassador for the State Department, a position he held until his death. Ultimately reconciling with the USOC, he also became its spokesman. In 1976 President Gerald Ford awarded Owens the Presidential Medal of Freedom. And upon Owens' death in 1980, President Jimmy Carter gave him a stirring eulogy: "Perhaps no athlete better symbolized the human struggle against tyranny, poverty, and racial bigotry. His work with young athletes, as an unofficial ambassador overseas, and as a spokesman for freedom, are a rich legacy to his fellow Americans."

"All we athletes get out of this Olympic business is a view out of a train or airplane window." —*Jesse Owens*

BIBLIOGRAPHY

Bass, Amy. *Not the Triumph but the Struggle: The 1968 Olympics and the Making of the Black Athlete.* Minneapolis: University of Minnesota Press, 2002.

Bernstein, Mark F. *Football: The Ivy League Origins of an American Obsession.* Philadelphia: University of Pennsylvania Press, 2001.

Davis, Benjamin J. *Communist Councilman from Harlem: Autobiographical Notes Written in a Federal Penitentiary.* New York: International Publishers, 1991.

Djata, Sundiata. *Blacks at the Net.* Syracuse, N.Y.: Syracuse University Press, 2006.

Fleischer, Nat. *Black Dynamite: Story of the Negro in Boxing.* New York: The Ring Athletic Library. Printed by C.J. O'Brien. 1938.

George, Nelson. *Elevating the Game: Black Men & Basketball.* Lincoln, Neb.: University of Nebraska Press, 1999.

Grimsley, Will. *Tennis: Its History, People and Events.* Englewood Cliffs, N.J.: Prentice-Hall, 1971.

Harris, Othello, Kirsch, George B., and Nolte, Claire E. *Encyclopedia of Ethnicity and Sports in the United States.* Westport, Conn.: Greenwood Press, 2000.

Henderson, Edwin Bancroft, with Miller, Patrick B. *Sport and the Color Line: Black Athletes and Race Relations in Twentieth-Century America.* New York: Routledge, 2004.

Hogan, Lawrence D. *Shades of Glory.* Washington, D.C.: National Geographic, 2006.

Holloway, John B. *Blackball Stars: Negro League Pioneers.* Westport, Conn.: Meckler Books, 1988.

Hotaling, Edward. *The Great Black Jockeys: The Lives and Times of the Men Who Dominated America's First National Sport.* Rocklin, Calif.: Forum, 1999.

Hotaling, Edward. *Wink: The Incredible Life and Epic Journey of Jimmy Winkfield.* New York: McGraw-Hill, 2005.

McDaniel, Pete. *Uneven Lies: The Heroic Story of African-Americans in Golf.* Greenwich, Conn.: American Golfer, 2000.

McGovern, Mike. *Amazing Athletes of the 20th Century.* New York: Checkmark Books, 2001.

Metcalfe, Henry. *A Game for All Races: An Illustrated History of the Negro Leagues.* New York: MetroBooks, 2000.

Miller, Patrick B., and Wiggins, David K. *Sport and the Color Line: Black Athletes and Race Relations in Twentieth-Century America.* Contributors. New York: Routledge, 2004.

Owens, Jesse. *The Jesse Owens Story.* New York: Putnam Publishing Group, 1970.

Robinson, Frazier, with Bauer, Paul. *Catching Dreams: My Life in the Negro Baseball Leagues.* Syracuse, N.Y.: Syracuse University Press, 1999.

Robinson, Sugar Ray, with Anderson, Dave. *The Sugar Ray Robinson Story.* Cambridge, Mass.: Da Capo Press, 1994.

Rogosi, Donn. *Invisible Men: Life in Baseball's Negro League.* New York: Atheneum, 1983.

Russell, William F., *Second Wind: The Memiors of an Opinionated Man.* New York: Random House, 1979.

Russell, William F., and McSweeny, William Francis. *Go Up for Glory.* New York: Coward, 1980.

Schaap, Jeremy. *Triumph: The Untold Story of Jesse Owens and Hitler's Olympics.* Boston: Houghton Mifflin, 2007

White, Sol. *White's History of Colored Base Ball With Other Documents of the Early Black Game, 1886-1936.* Lincoln, Neb.: University of Nebraska Press, 1995.

Wiggins, David K. *Glory Bound: Black Athletes in a White America.* Syracuse, N.Y.: Syracuse University Press, 1997.

Woolum, Janet. *Outstanding Women Athletes: Who They Are and How They Influenced Sports in America.* Phoenix, Ariz.: Oryx Press, 1998.

ACKNOWLEDGMENTS

This book would not have been possible without the hard work, support, and perseverance of so many people. First, we'd like to thank ESPN, and especially Keith Clinkscales and Gary Hoenig, for turning our dream of writing a book into a reality. We cannot thank Tony Dungy enough for writing the Foreword and sharing his wisdom. Thanks to our masterly editor and sports historian, Steve Wulf, who always had time to share a few amazing sports stories along the way. Thank you, Richard Rosen, for making our words sing. To Sandy DeShong and John Glenn, thank you for stewarding the book through the publishing process and patiently explaining every step along the way. Thank you to our colleagues at Ballantine Books, who embraced the project with open arms. Thank you to photo editor extraordinaire Sara Shaoul, who left no stone unturned until she found the perfect picture; to Ronda Racha Penrice, who helped us in the early stages of the grueling research process; and much gratitude to Amanda Angel, whose diligent fact-checking kept us on our toes. And a huge thank you to Henry Lee for his elegant design and vision for the book. He's the best graphic designer we could have had on this project.

PHOTOGRAPHY & ILLUSTRATION CREDITS

ABOUT THE AUTHORS

ROXANNE JONES is one of the founding editors of *ESPN The Magazine* and helped to create such ESPN programs as *Cold Pizza* and the Emmy-nominated *The Life*. A former editor at the *Philadelphia Inquirer* and New York *Daily News*, she has served on the boards of the National Association of Black Journalists and St. Mary-of-the-Woods College in Terre Haute, Indiana. In addition, she is the recipient of the 2010 Woman of the Year Award given by Women in Sports & Entertainment. She and her family live in Brooklyn, New York.

JESSIE PAOLUCCI got her start in sports journalism as a writer-reporter for *Total Sports*. She was one of the founding editors of *ESPN The Magazine*, where she oversaw several departments, including "The Jump," which was nominated for Best Magazine Section by the American Society of Magazine Editors in 2005. She was deputy editor at *Budget Living* magazine and served as a consultant and producer for ESPN's Content Group. Jessie is currently a freelance writer, editor, and web producer and is developing an online nonprofit for young volunteers. She lives in Brooklyn, New York.